The MAILBOX®

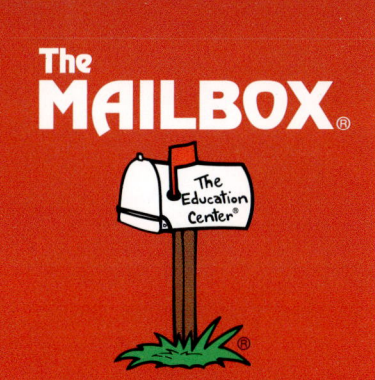

Nonfiction Comprehension Builders

Grades 2–5

THE BEST OF The MAILBOX® Bookbag® MAGAZINE

The best nonfiction passages and related activities from the 2003–2007 issues of *The Mailbox® BOOKBAG®* magazine

Reinforces 50 different skills, including

- Predicting
- Questioning
- Comparing and contrasting
- Main idea and supporting details
- Vocabulary
- Drawing conclusions
- Fact and opinion
- Summarizing
- Context clues

Managing Editor: Jenny Chapman

Editorial Team: Becky S. Andrews, Diane Badden, Kimberley Bruck, Karen A. Brudnak, Kitty Campbell, Lynette Dickerson, Theresa Lewis Goode, Tazmen Hansen, Marsha Heim, Lori Z. Henry, Debra Liverman, Dorothy C. McKinney, Thad H. McLaurin, Sharon Murphy, Jennifer Nunn, Mark Rainey, Hope Rodgers, Rebecca Saunders, Zane Williard

Skills Index on page 112!

www.themailbox.com

©2009 The Mailbox® Books
All rights reserved.
ISBN10 #1-56234-878-7 • ISBN13 #978-156234-878-6

Except as provided for herein, no part of this publication may be reproduced or transmitted in any form or by any means, electronic or mechanical, including photocopying, recording, or storing in any information storage and retrieval system or electronic online bulletin board, without prior written permission from The Education Center, Inc. Permission is given to the original purchaser to reproduce patterns and reproducibles for individual classroom use only and not for resale or distribution. Reproduction for an entire school or school system is prohibited. Please direct written inquiries to The Education Center, Inc., P.O. Box 9753, Greensboro, NC 27429-0753. The Education Center®, *The Mailbox*®, the mailbox/post/grass logo, and The Mailbox Book Company® are registered trademarks of The Education Center, Inc. All other brand or product names are trademarks or registered trademarks of their respective companies.

Manufactured in the United States
10 9 8 7 6 5 4 3 2 1

Table of Contents

What's Inside 3

Nonfiction Topic	Unit Title	Page
Bats and rats	Bats! Rats!	4
Skateboards	Roll On!	8
Giant squid	A Sea Monster?	13
Juggling	Let's Juggle!	17
Bikes	Anything But Ordinary	21
Games	Wacky Games Kids Play	25
Poison dart frogs	Wanted: Frog Facts	29
Ants	The "Ant-ernet"	33
Drawing	How to Draw a Cartoon Character	38
Opossums	Pouch Potatoes	42
Video games	On the Record: Video Games	46
Good luck charms	Just for Luck!	50
Jon Scieszka	Jon Scieszka	54
Sharks	Shark Sense	58
Piranhas	Eating Machines	62
Pirate ship	What About the *Whydah*?	66
Rain forest creature	In Search of the Strange	70
Abandoned ships	Phantom Ships	74
Presidential pets	1600 "Pet-sylvania" Avenue	78
J. K. Rowling	A Magical Pen	81
Parasites	Bloodsucking Pests	85
Mimicry	Hiding in Plain View	89
Roald Dahl	An Accidental Writer	93
Rosa Parks	Taking a Seat for Change	96
Mount St. Helens	Two Men and a Mountain	100
Tracking a hurricane	Without Warning	103
Mammoths and mastodons	The Riddle of the Bones	107

Answer Keys 110

Skills Index 112

What's Inside

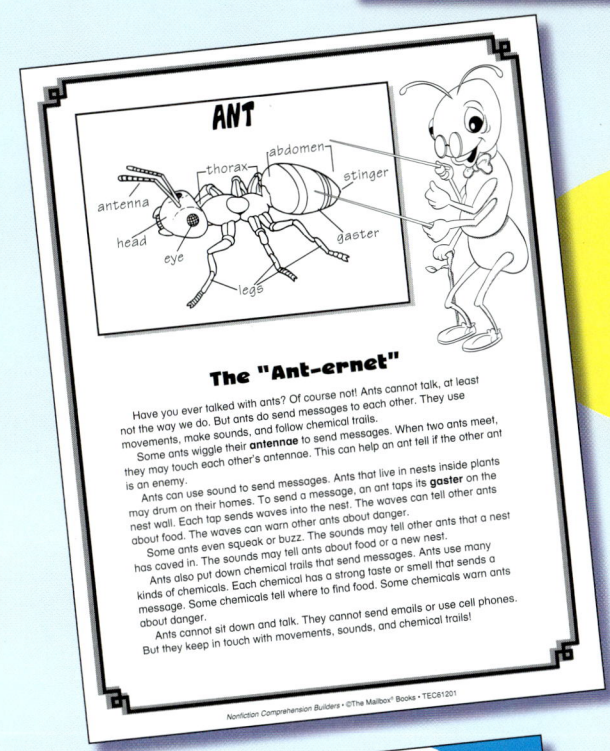

27 high-interest nonfiction passages

More than **100** activities and reproducibles to boost key comprehension skills and strategies!

"Bats! Rats!"

by Bonnie Franz, Staten Island, NY

Activating Prior Knowledge

Before reading the passage on page 6, have each student fill out the top of page 7 to share what he knows about bats and rats. Also guide the child to list something he wonders about bats or rats or both. After reading, have the child add information from the passage and review his "I wonder…" statement. If he finds an answer in the passage, have him record it on the paper's flip side. If he does not find an answer, guide him to further research his question and share the answer with the class.

Comparing and Contrasting

After reading the passage, have each pair of students stack two sheets of unlined paper so that the edges are about one inch apart. Next, have the pair fold, staple, and label its booklet as shown. Then guide the duo to reread the passage, writing and drawing notes on the labeled pages. Follow up by having each child complete a copy of the bottom half of page 7 to compare and contrast bats and rats.

Rhyming

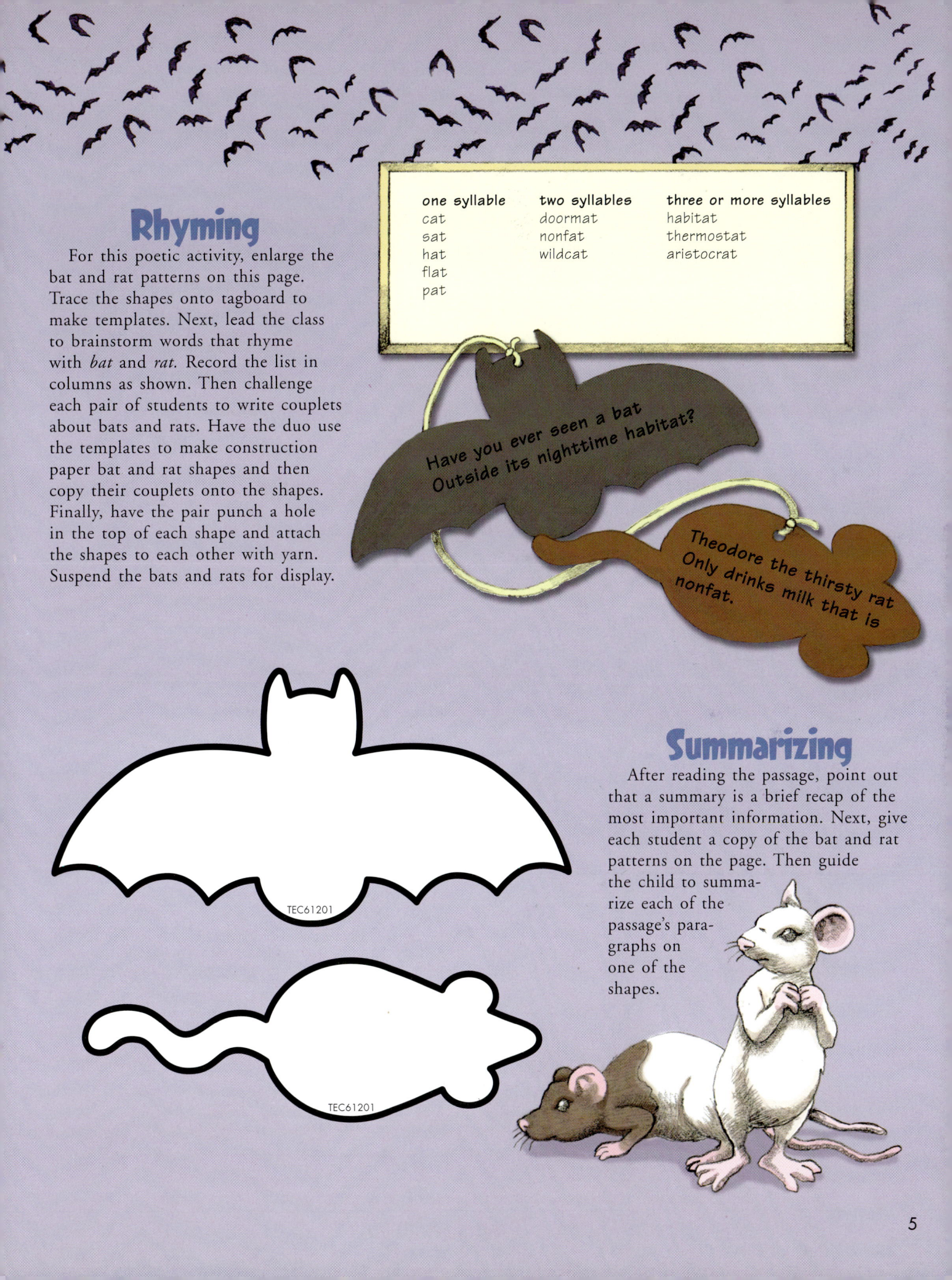

For this poetic activity, enlarge the bat and rat patterns on this page. Trace the shapes onto tagboard to make templates. Next, lead the class to brainstorm words that rhyme with *bat* and *rat*. Record the list in columns as shown. Then challenge each pair of students to write couplets about bats and rats. Have the duo use the templates to make construction paper bat and rat shapes and then copy their couplets onto the shapes. Finally, have the pair punch a hole in the top of each shape and attach the shapes to each other with yarn. Suspend the bats and rats for display.

one syllable	two syllables	three or more syllables
cat	doormat	habitat
sat	nonfat	thermostat
hat	wildcat	aristocrat
flat		
pat		

Have you ever seen a bat
Outside its nighttime habitat?

Theodore the thirsty rat
Only drinks milk that is nonfat.

Summarizing

After reading the passage, point out that a summary is a brief recap of the most important information. Next, give each student a copy of the bat and rat patterns on the page. Then guide the child to summarize each of the passage's paragraphs on one of the shapes.

TEC61201
TEC61201

5

Bats! Rats!

Bats and rats have rhyming names. But they are not the same animals. After all, bats fly, and rats walk. Rats are rodents. Bats are not. Most bats eat insects or fruit. Rats eat just about anything. Bats sleep upside down. Rats do not. Yet bats and rats are alike in some ways.

Bats are mammals. Rats are mammals. They both have fur. They are both warm-blooded. Their babies drink milk. Bats and rats both hunt for food at night. Most bats and nearly all rats see well in the dark. They both have great hearing too. In fact, they hear much better than we do! These mammals with rhyming names are different in many ways, but in some ways, they are alike.

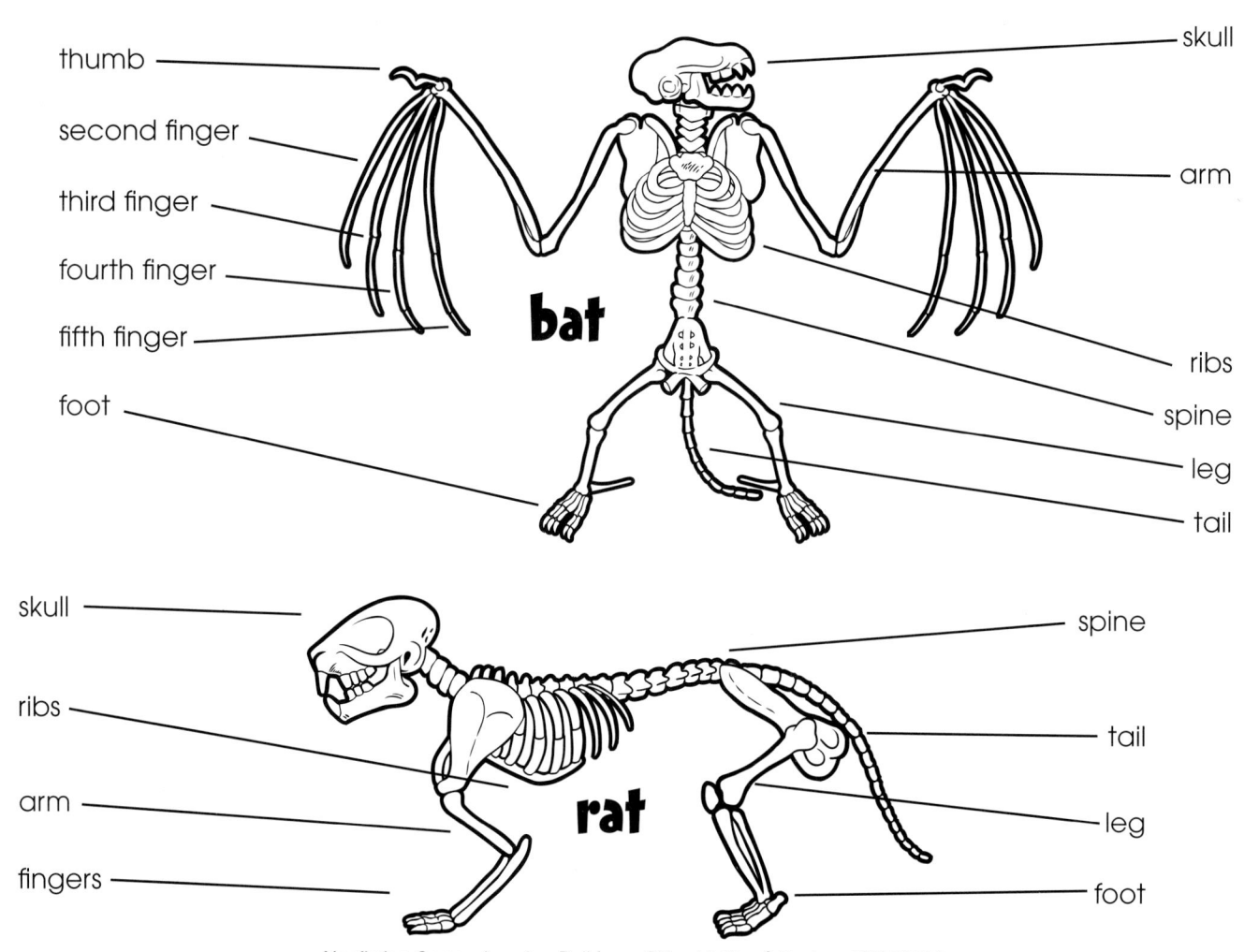

bat

- thumb
- second finger
- third finger
- fourth finger
- fifth finger
- foot
- skull
- arm
- ribs
- spine
- leg
- tail

rat

- skull
- ribs
- arm
- fingers
- spine
- tail
- leg
- foot

Nonfiction Comprehension Builders • ©The Mailbox® Books • TEC61201

Note to the teacher: Use this reading selection with the activities on pages 4, 5, and 7.

Name _____
Activating prior knowledge

What a Pair!

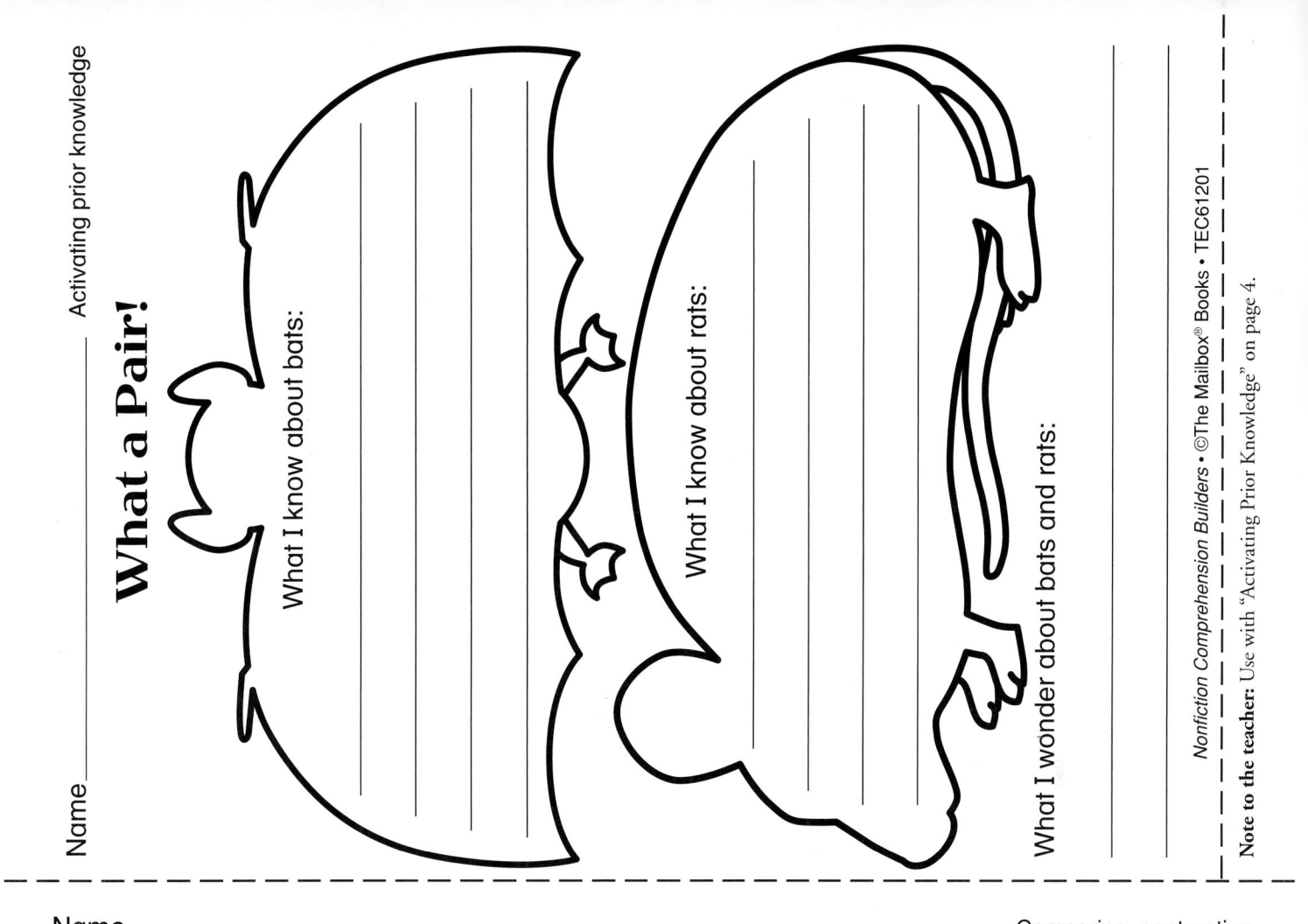

What I know about bats:

What I know about rats:

What I wonder about bats and rats:

Nonfiction Comprehension Builders • ©The Mailbox® Books • TEC61201

Note to the teacher: Use with "Activating Prior Knowledge" on page 4.

Name _____ Comparing, contrasting

All About Bats and Rats

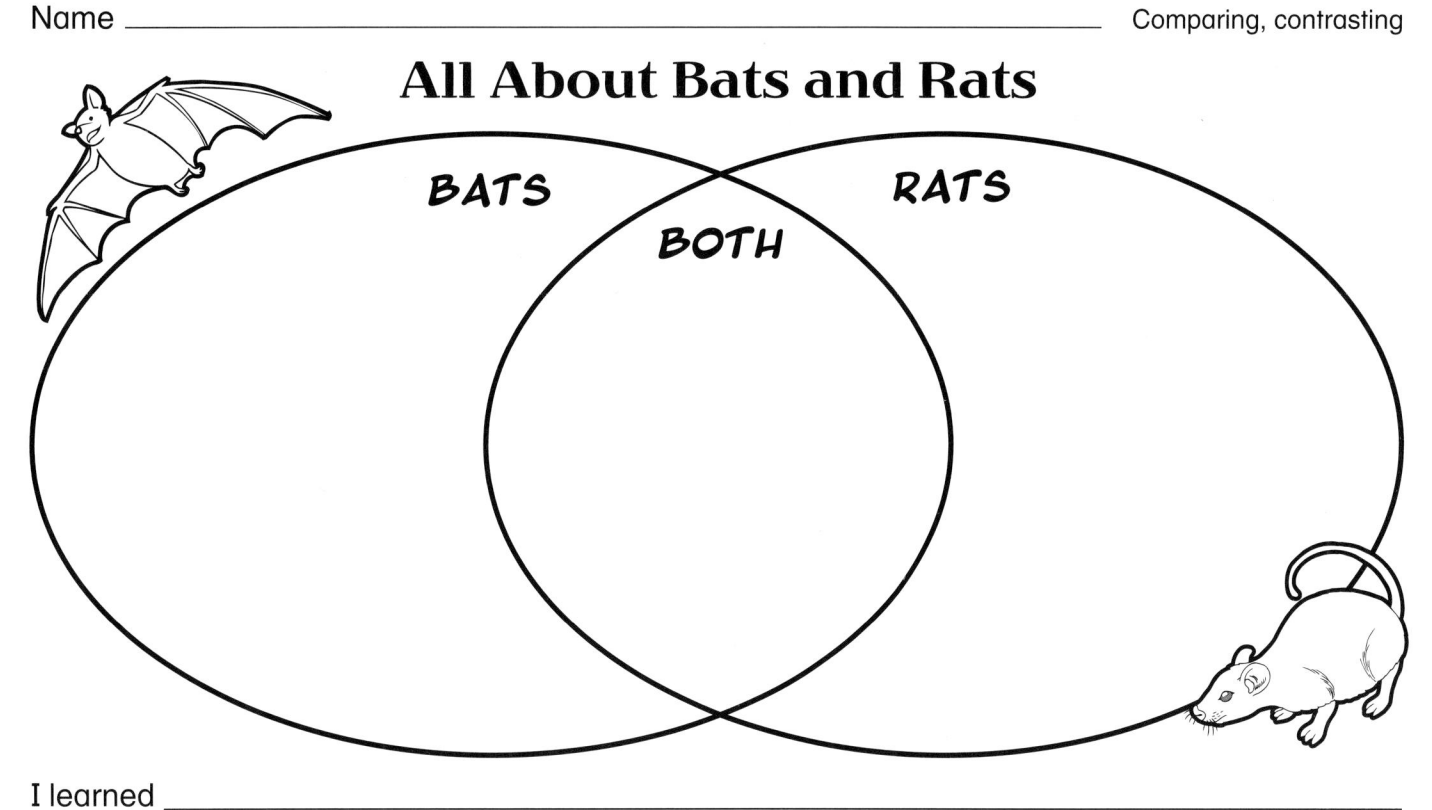

BATS   BOTH   RATS

I learned _____

_____

Nonfiction Comprehension Builders • ©The Mailbox® Books • TEC61201

Note to the teacher: Use with "Comparing and Contrasting" on page 4.

7

"Roll On!"

by Angela Rood, Dyersburg, TN

Establishing a Reading Purpose

Before reading, have each student fold a sheet of paper in half vertically and trim it to make a skateboard shape. Next, the child opens up the skateboard shape, draws a line along the fold, and labels each side as shown. On the left side, the youngster shares what he knows about skateboarding using pictures and words and then, on the right side, he lists questions he has about skateboarding. After reading the passage, each child records what he learned about skateboarding using pictures and words on the skateboard shape's flip side.

What I Know About Skateboarding
Tony Hawk is the best skater ever! I can do an ollie.
I'm trying to learn how to do a kickflip.

What I Want to Know
Who invented skateboards?
When did people start skateboarding?
What is the hardest trick?

What I Learned
A long time ago skateboards were made with boards and roller skates.
New kinds of wheels are better for doing tricks.
Now skaters do all kinds of tricks.

Compound Words

Here's an activity that reminds students to look for words they know when they see long words. First, have each pair of students write a compound word from the passage (see the list) on a web as shown. Next, guide the pair to identify each word's parts and then use the parts to figure out the word's meaning. Repeat with each word in the list. Then have the partners use their work to help them read the passage.

- skateboard
- sidewalk
- became
- handrails

skateboard → skate + board → a board that you can skate on

High-Frequency Words

For this game, make a copy of page 11 for each student plus one extra copy. Cut apart the word cards on the extra copy and place the cards in a small container. Next, have each student cut apart his word cards, arrange them on his gameboard, and glue them down. To play, give each child a handful of game markers. Then draw a word card and read it aloud. Guide each youngster to find the word on his gameboard and put a marker on that space. Repeat until a student marks four spaces in a row. Congratulate that child, have students clear their boards, and then play again!

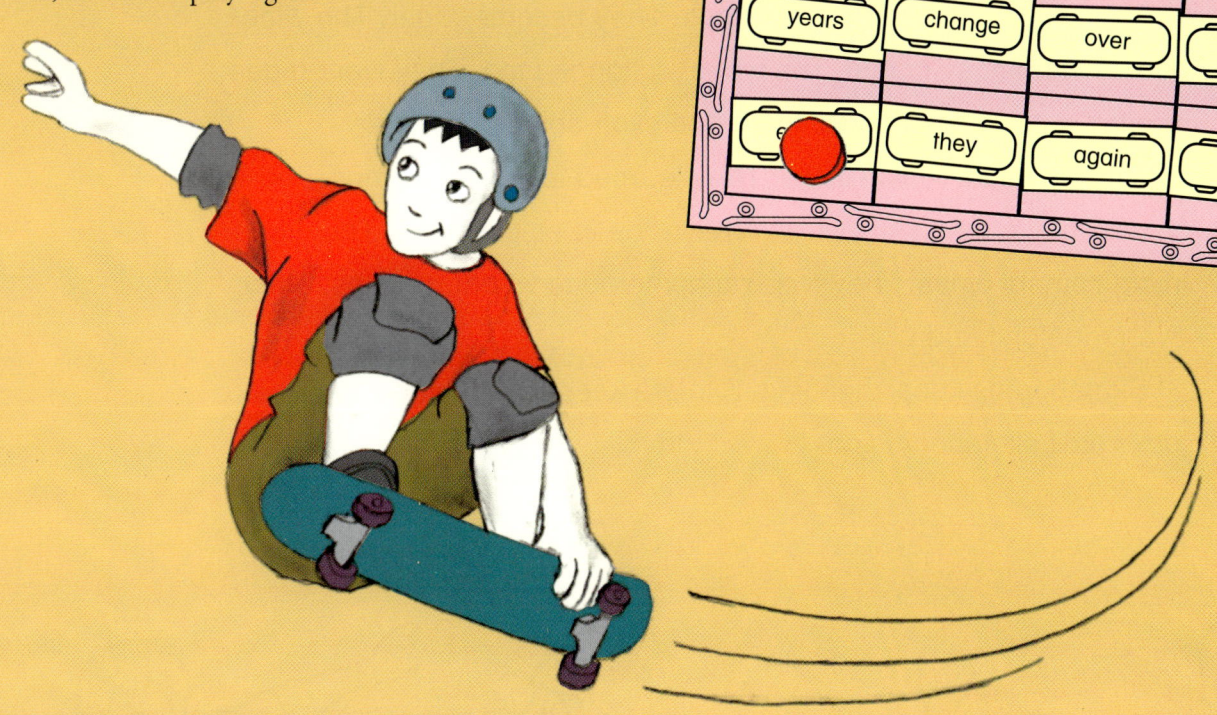

The first skateboards were made from toy scooters.
Riding a skateboard is a lot of fun.

Fact and Opinion

Begin this critical-thinking activity by writing on the board the sentences shown. Read aloud the first sentence. Point to your head and explain that the sentence is a true statement. Then read aloud the second sentence. Point to your heart and explain that the statement tells how someone feels. Guide each small group of students to skim the selection and then write a fact and an opinion about skateboarding. Have each group share its statements. After each statement, challenge students to point to their heads or to their hearts to show which statements are facts and which statements are opinions. Follow up by having each student complete a copy of page 12.

ROLL ON!

Skateboards have been around for over 60 years. But they have changed a lot. First, they were made from toy scooters. Next, they were made from steel-wheeled roller skates and skinny boards. Riding a skateboard was like surfing on the sidewalk.

Then skateboards changed again. They became wider. The wider boards were easy to ride. The wheels changed too. They were made of hard plastic. This plastic made the skateboards go faster.

Skaters began doing tricks. They learned to do flips, jumps, and spins. They rode on sidewalks. They rode in empty pools. They rode in big cement pipes. They rode on homemade wooden ramps. They even rode on handrails.

Skateboards keep changing. Skaters keep learning new tricks. It looks as if skateboards are here to stay!

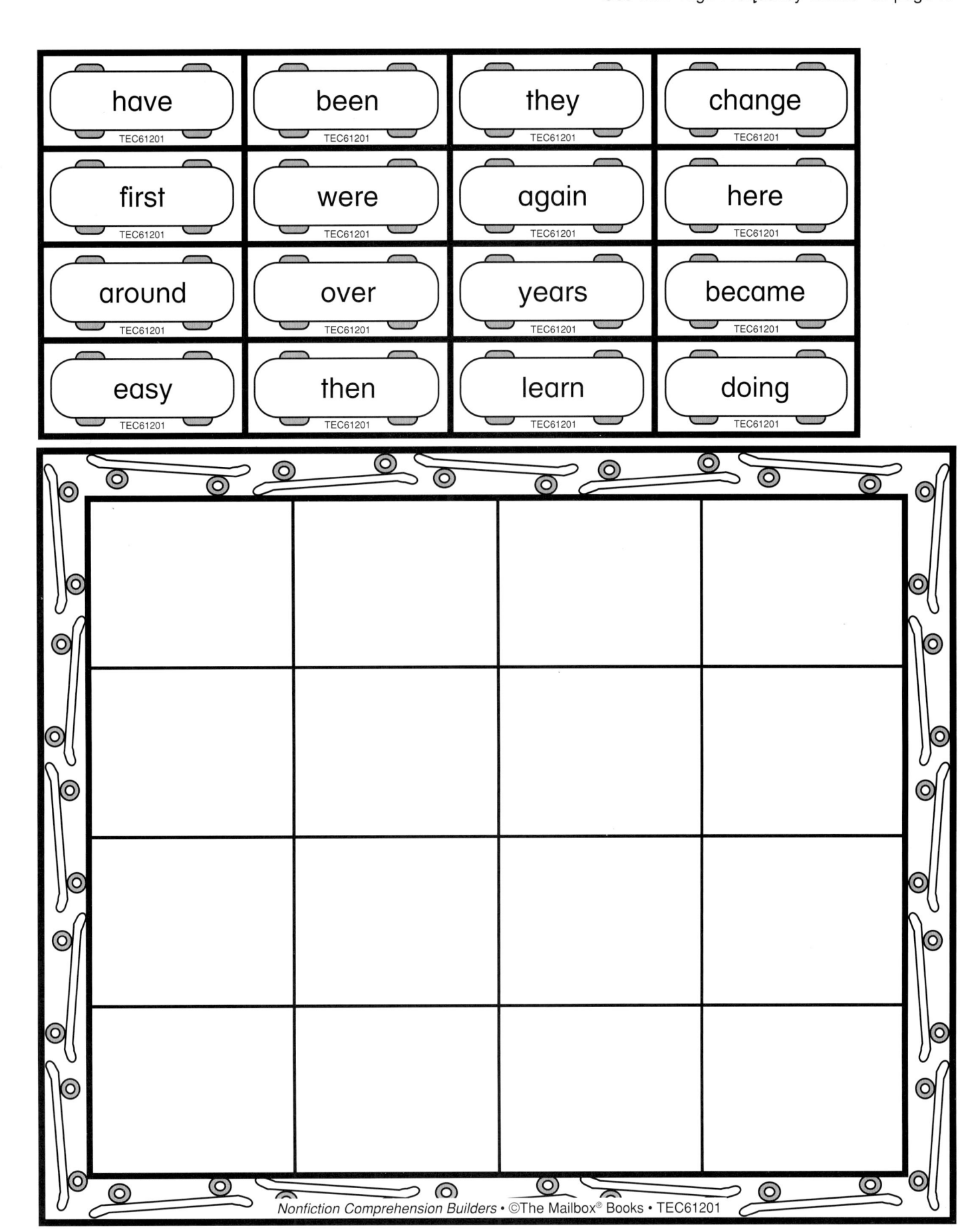

Word Cards and Gameboard
Use with "High-Frequency Words" on page 9.

have	been	they	change
first	were	again	here
around	over	years	became
easy	then	learn	doing

Name _____   Fact and opinion

On a Roll!

If the sentence is a fact, shade the box below *fact*.
If the sentence is an opinion, shade the box below *opinion*.

		Fact	Opinion
1.	The best skateboards are skinny.	S	O
2.	Skateboards have been around for over 60 years.	K	G
3.	Skateboarding is the world's greatest sport.	B	A
4.	Skateboards used to be made with roller skates.	W	J
5.	Skateboards have changed a lot.	D	M
6.	It is easy to do tricks on a skateboard.	T	R
7.	There are many kinds of tricks.	L	C
8.	The easiest trick to do is a jump.	F	E
9.	Steel wheels are too noisy.	V	H
10.	Skateboards with hard plastic wheels can go fast.	Y	P

How did the skater make straight As?
To find out, write the colored letters on the matching lines below.

The skater ___ ___ ___ ___ ___ " ___ ___ ___ ___ ___ - ___ "
           4   1   6   2   8   5   4   9   8   8   7   10

___ ___ ___ ___ !
 9   3   6   5

Nonfiction Comprehension Builders • ©The Mailbox® Books • TEC61201 • Key p. 110

12   **Note to the teacher:** Use with "Fact and Opinion" on page 9.

"A Sea Monster?"

*with ideas by Terry Healy, Eugene Field Elementary
Manhattan, KS*

Building Background Knowledge

Before reading the selection on page 15, share with students basic facts about squid, such as those shown. Then guide each child to color the squid diagram on a copy of page 16 as directed and keep the diagram handy while he reads the selection.

Squid Facts
- Squid have no backbones. Their bodies are soft.
- Squid belong to the same animal group as octopuses.
- Most squid have eight arms and two tentacles. Their arms and tentacles have suckers that they use to hold on to their food.
- Squid have an ink sac that squirts dark liquid. When a squid is in danger, it squirts the dark liquid. Then it swims away.

Visualizing

To help students comprehend the selection, have each child fold a sheet of unlined paper in thirds and label the sections as shown. Next, read aloud the first paragraph and guide each child to draw in the first section the images she pictures as you read. Repeat for the second and third paragraphs. Then review with students that some details are more important than others. Guide each student to review her sketches and circle the drawings that most help her understand the selection. Finally, have the child use those images to draw on another sheet of paper an illustration that summarizes the selection.

13

Fluency

Help students read in meaningful phrases rather than word by word. To begin, code a copy of the selection on page 15 with marks that reinforce proper phrasing. Place the coded page at a center along with a tape recorder and a blank tape. Next, guide each student to practice reading the selection into the recorder. Then have him listen to himself and compare his phrasing to the coded page.

A Sea Monster?

People used to tell tales of giant sea monsters. They told tales of monsters that crushed ships. They told tales of monsters that attacked whales. Those tales may have been about giant squid. Giant squid are real. And they are big! But they aren't monsters.

Giant squid can grow to be about 60 feet long. That's longer than a school bus! People might have thought giant squid were monsters because of their huge eyes. Each one of a giant squid's eyes is as big as a person's head. Giant squid need big eyes to see in dark water. They live deep in the ocean where there isn't much light.

Giant squid hunt other kinds of squid and fish. But they are also hunted! Sperm whales eat giant squid. Giant squid fight the whales to protect themselves. But they don't attack ships. They don't attack whales, and they don't attack people.

Giant squid are, after all, very big sea creatures. But they are not sea monsters.

Skimming

Give each student a copy of page 15. Explain that you are going to begin reading somewhere in the first paragraph and that each child should read as quickly as she can to find the spot where you are reading. Tell students that as soon as each child finds the spot, she should read aloud with you. Then choose a spot in the first paragraph and begin reading aloud. Read the whole paragraph to give students time to catch up with you. Repeat with the second and third paragraphs and then pick a spot from anywhere in the selection and guide students to skim the page and catch up with you.

Narrative Writing

After reading the selection, have each child imagine that he sees a live giant squid while he is exploring in a deep-sea submersible. Guide the child to draw what he might see and then write a story that describes the adventure. Have each student write his final copy on paper trimmed so that it resembles a giant squid. Then post students' work on a bulletin board decorated to look like the ocean and titled "Deep-Sea Narratives."

Mark

We went down and down in the ocean. There was a shipwreck on the bottom. We wondered if a giant squid would live inside the shipwreck. There were all kinds of little fish swimming in and out of the shipwreck. All of a sudden, we saw a long tentacle try to grab a fish. The fish got away and the tentacle reached out farther and farther. We saw a bunch of arms and the edge of a huge glassy eye! The eye looked right at us. It was huge! Then the squid ducked back behind the shipwreck and took off. We waited for a while, but the giant squid did not come back. So we headed back up to the surface.

A Sea Monster?

People used to tell tales of giant sea monsters. They told tales of monsters that crushed ships. They told tales of monsters that attacked whales. Those tales may have been about giant squid. Giant squid are real. And they are big! But they aren't monsters.

Giant squid can grow to be about 60 feet long. That's longer than a school bus! People might have thought giant squid were monsters because of their huge eyes. Each one of a giant squid's eyes is as big as a person's head. Giant squid need big eyes to see in dark water. They live deep in the ocean where there isn't much light.

Giant squid hunt other kinds of squid and fish. But they are also hunted! Sperm whales eat giant squid. Giant squid fight the whales to protect themselves. But they don't attack ships. They don't attack whales, and they don't attack people.

Giant squid are, after all, very big sea creatures. But they are not sea monsters.

Note to the teacher: Use this reading selection with pages 13, 14, and 16.

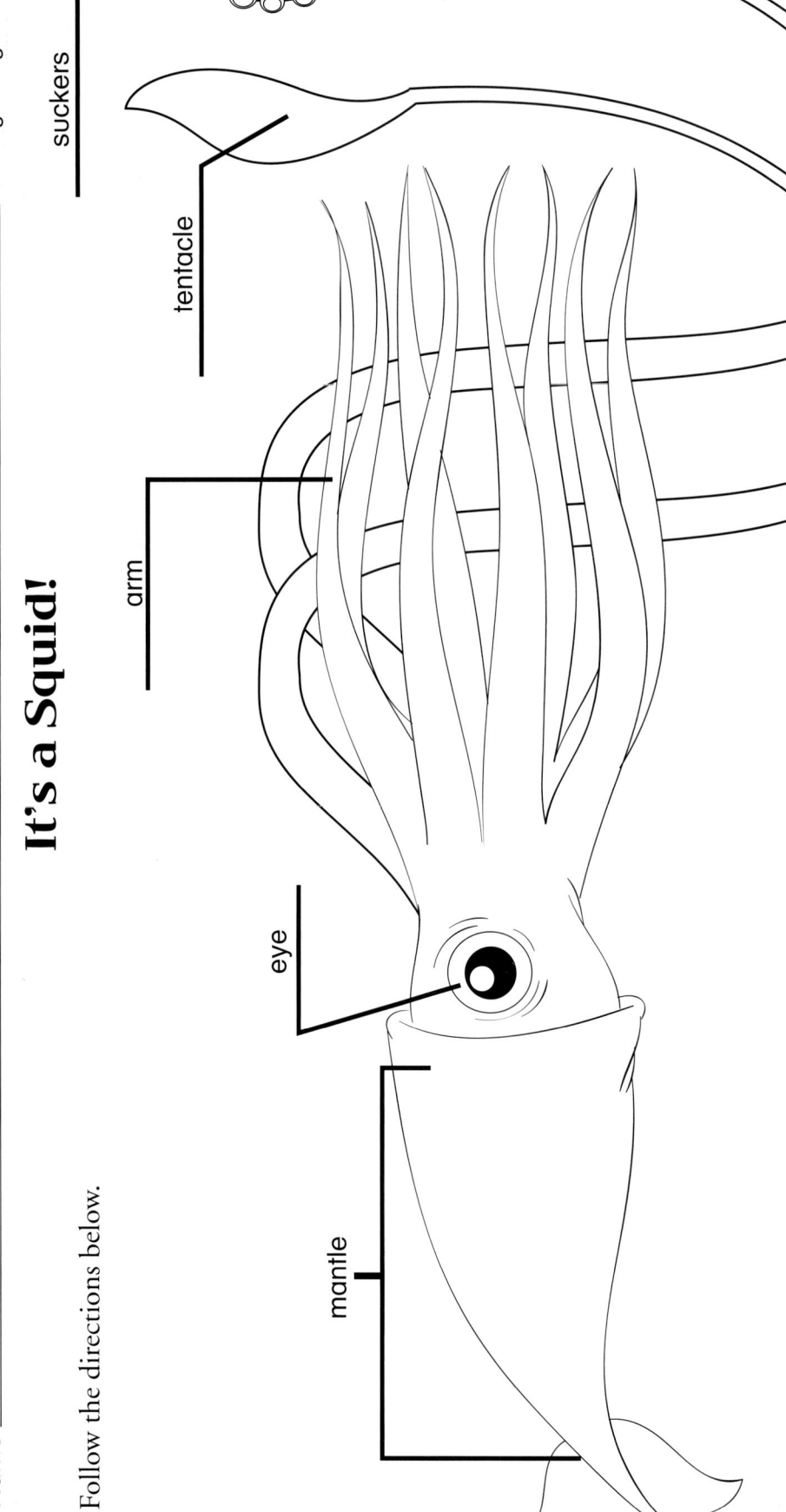

Name _____

Building background knowledge

It's a Squid!

Follow the directions below.

suckers

tentacle

arm

eye

mantle

1. Color the arms orange.
2. Color the tentacles green.
3. Color the eye brown.
4. Color the suckers blue.
5. Color the mantle red.
6. Color the rest of the squid yellow.

Note to the teacher: Use with "Building Background Knowledge" on page 13.

Nonfiction Comprehension Builders • ©The Mailbox® Books • TEC61201 • Key p. 110

"Let's Juggle!"

by Cynthia Holcomb, San Angelo, TX

Activating Prior Knowledge

Use this step-by-step plan to get students thinking about the selection before they read. To begin, give each pair of students a copy of page 20 and have the duo complete Steps 1 through 4. Then give the partners a copy of the selection on page 19 and guide them to complete Steps 5 and 6.

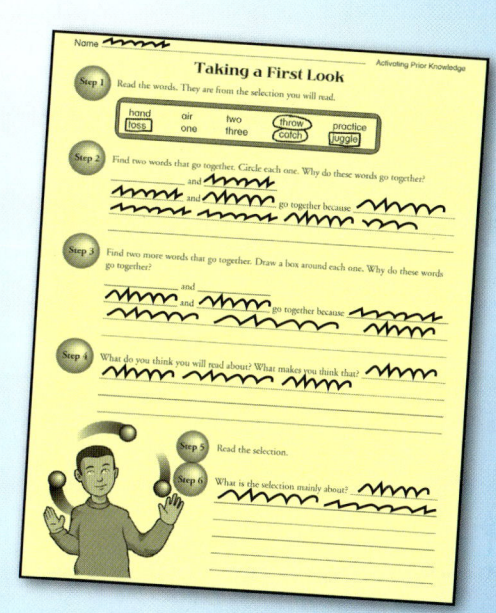

Vocabulary

For this exploration, have each student fold a sheet of paper in half two times. Next, have the child open the paper and fold each corner toward the center fold as shown. Then guide each student to follow the steps below for one vocabulary word (see the list). Finally, have each child share his work with a group of students who explored different words.

Steps:
1. Write the vocabulary word in the center.
2. Write "What I Know" on one flap. Fold back the flap and tell what you know about the word.
3. Write "What It Means" on one flap. Look up the word in a dictionary. Fold back the flap and write the word's meaning.
4. Write "Picture" on one flap. Fold back the flap and draw a picture that illustrates the word.
5. Write "How It's Used" on one flap. Fold back the flap and tell how the word is used in the selection.

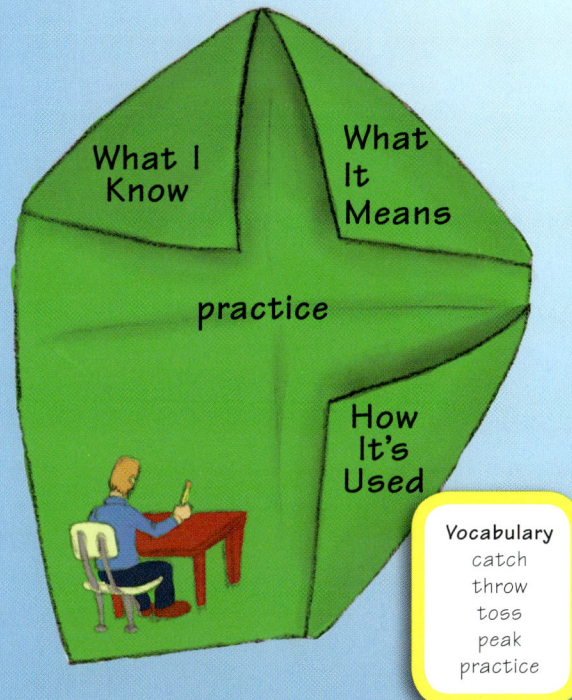

Vocabulary
catch
throw
toss
peak
practice

Following Directions

To begin, gather several clean socks and roll each one into a ball. Next, give each student a copy of page 19. Have the child skim Step 1, circle the number of balls she needs, and take a balled-up sock. Guide the child to read the step and then practice tossing and catching the sock for a set amount of time. Next, have her write about her experience on a ball-shaped cutout. As time allows, have the student continue skimming, reading, practicing, and describing her experiences, one step at a time. When each child finishes, have her personalize a construction paper cover and staple her juggling journal together. To display, post a copy of the selection on a board titled "Let's Juggle!" Then add each child's journal.

Making Inferences

Divide students into small groups and have each group read the selection on a copy of page 19. Next, draw and label a four-column chart, as shown, and give each group four sticky notes. Guide each group to brainstorm ideas for each category. Then have each team post its notes in the appropriate columns to share its ideas. Follow up with a class discussion, encouraging students to toss around even more ideas!

Let's Juggle!

Step 1: Start with one ball. Toss it into the air and catch it with your other hand. Practice until you throw the ball the same way each time.

Step 2: Next, add another ball. Hold one ball in each hand. Toss the first ball. When it is at its *peak,* or highest point, throw the second ball. Practice until you can toss and catch two balls.

Step 3: When you can throw and catch two balls, add a third one. Hold two balls in one hand and one in the other. Toss the first ball. When it is at its peak, throw the second ball. When the second ball is at its peak, toss the third one. Don't try to catch the balls at first. Just get used to throwing each ball at the right time.

Step 4: When you are used to tossing all three balls, try to catch them. Practice until you can throw and catch three balls.

Step 5: Now you are ready to juggle. Start by tossing and catching the three balls. When the third ball is at its peak, throw the first ball into the air again. Then just keep going. That's juggling!

Name _____   Activating Prior Knowledge

Taking a First Look

Step 1 Read the words. They are from the selection you will read.

hand	air	two	throw	practice
toss	one	three	catch	juggle

Step 2 Find two words that go together. Circle each one. Why do these words go together?

_____ and _____ go together because _____
_____
_____

Step 3 Find two more words that go together. Draw a box around each one. Why do these words go together?

_____ and _____ go together because _____
_____
_____

Step 4 What do you think you will read about? What makes you think that? _____
_____
_____
_____

Step 5 Read the selection.

Step 6 What is the selection mainly about? _____
_____
_____
_____
_____

Nonfiction Comprehension Builders • ©The Mailbox® Books • TEC61201

Note to the teacher: Use with "Activating Prior Knowledge" on page 17.

"Anything But Ordinary"

by Kim Minafo, Dillard Drive Elementary, Raleigh, NC

Using Context Clues

Before reading the passage on page 23, give each student a copy of the cloze paragraph on the bottom half of page 22. Then guide the child to predict two words for each space and write his guesses in the helmets at the bottom of the page. After he records his guesses, lead each student to choose the word that best fits in each space and write it in. Then have the child read the paragraph to make sure it makes sense, making changes as necessary. After discussing students' work, have each child read the actual paragraph on a copy of page 23.

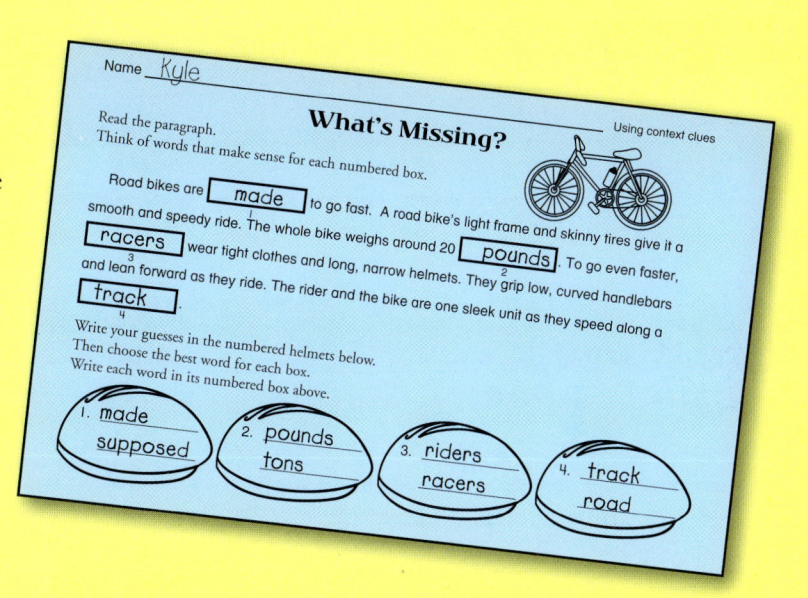

Compare and Contrast Key Words

To begin, label a transparent copy of the organizer on page 24 with "Comparing Words" and "Contrasting Words" as shown. Next, lead students to brainstorm words or phrases that signal comparing or contrasting text. Record students' ideas on the organizer. Then guide each child to read the passage on a copy of page 23 and highlight each comparing or contrasting key word or phrase she finds. Follow up by having each child compare road racing bikes and BMX bikes on a copy of page 24.

Questioning

For this modified game show activity, have each small group of students reread the passage on page 23. Also give each team six index cards. Next, read aloud the first answer below. Guide each group to write a question that matches the answer. Then have the groups read aloud their questions. Award one point for each question that matches the answer and then repeat for the remaining answers. Declare the team with the most points the winner.

Answers
1. A road bike has a light frame to help it go fast.
2. Road bikes are built to go fast, but BMX bikes are built to be strong.
3. A road bike weighs about 20 pounds.
4. BMX riders make high jumps and sharp turns.
5. Road bikes and BMX bikes are both light bikes.
6. BMX riders make high jumps and can crash when they land.

Possible Questions
1. Why does a road bike have a light frame?
2. How are road bikes and BMX bikes built differently?
3. How much does a road bike weigh?
4. Why do BMX bikes have to be strong?
5. How are road bikes and BMX bikes alike?
6. Why do BMX riders need sturdy helmets?

Name _____ Using context clues

What's Missing?

Read the paragraph.
Think of words that make sense for each numbered box.

   Road bikes are [___1___] to go fast. A road bike's light frame and skinny tires give it a smooth and speedy ride. The whole bike weighs around 20 [___2___]. To go even faster, [___3___] wear tight clothes and long, narrow helmets. They grip low, curved handlebars and lean forward as they ride. The rider and the bike are one sleek unit as they speed along a [___4___].

Write your guesses in the numbered helmets below.
Then choose the best word for each box.
Write each word in its numbered box above.

1. _____
2. _____
3. _____
4. _____

Nonfiction Comprehension Builders • ©The Mailbox® Books • TEC61201

22   Note to the teacher: Use with "Using Context Clues" on page 21.

ANYTHING BUT ORDINARY

Both road racing bikes and BMX bikes are built for extreme sports.

Road bikes are built to go fast. A road bike's light frame and skinny tires give it a smooth and speedy ride. The whole bike weighs around 20 pounds. To go even faster, racers wear tight clothes and long, narrow helmets. They grip low, curved handlebars and lean forward as they ride. The rider and the bike are one sleek unit as they speed along a course.

BMX bikes, on the other hand, are built to be strong. Their riders have to be able to make high jumps and sharp turns. Like a road bike, a BMX bike is light. But it has a strong frame. Its tires are small and wide. The handlebars have an extra brace for strength. The bike has pads, and the riders wear padded clothing. BMX riders can fall or crash when they make high jumps. Sturdy helmets are a must for BMX riders.

Modern road bikes and BMX bikes are anything but ordinary.

Name _____

Wheel Comparisons

"Wacky Games Kids Play"

by Stephanie Affinito, Glen Falls, NY

- Games have rules.
- There is a winner.
- I play Marco Polo at the pool.
- We have lots of math games.
- I play games on my computer.

Activating Prior Knowledge

Show students that they're ahead of the game by reminding them how much they already know. Before reading the passage on page 27, draw a gameboard path on the board. Then guide each student to share a different fact about games children play. Record each response on a gameboard space. After reading, challenge students to share even more facts about games kids play.

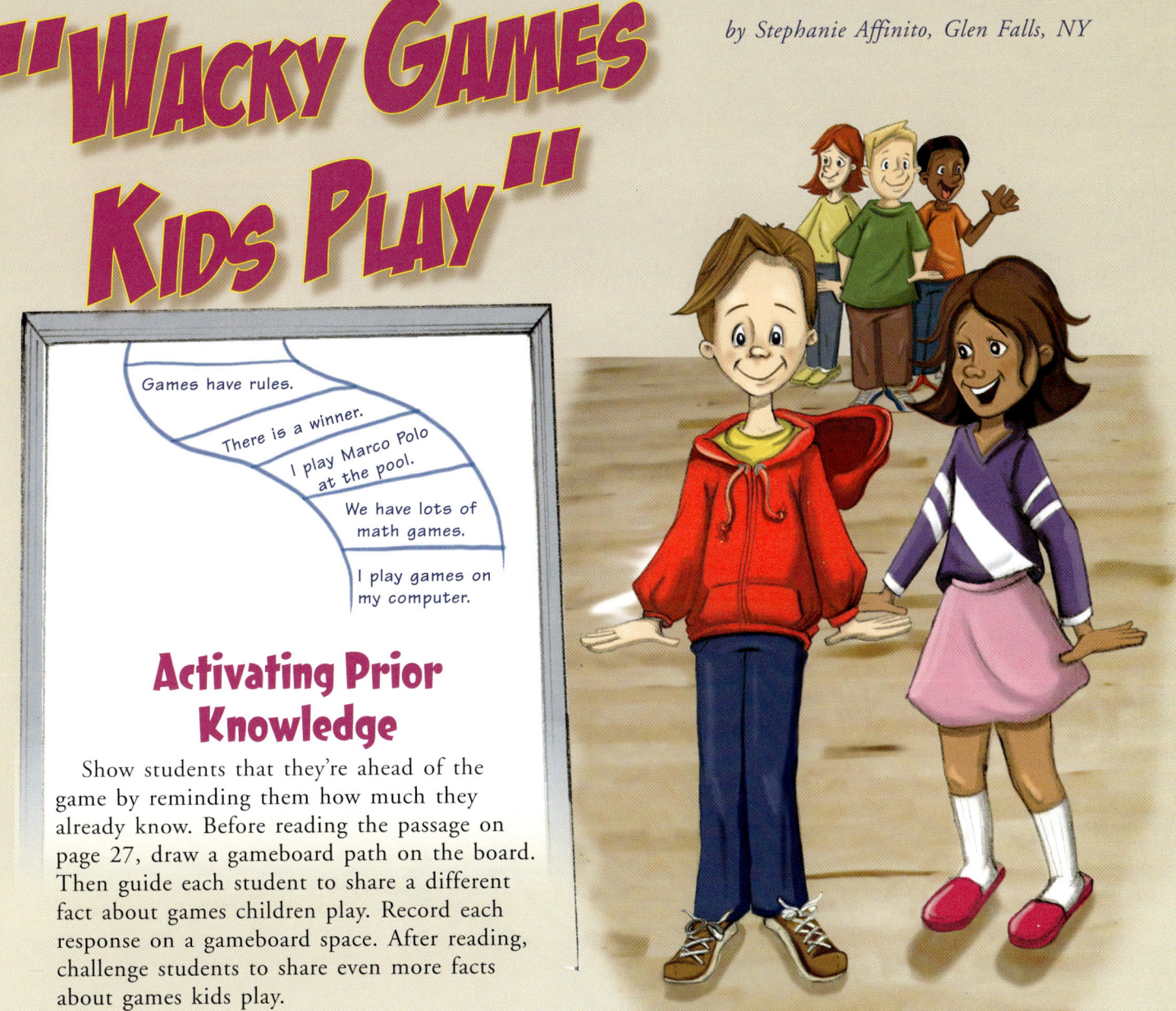

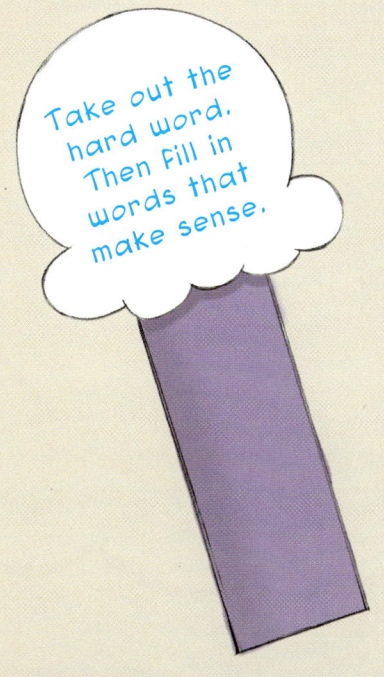

Take out the hard word. Then fill in words that make sense.

Using Context Clues

Make a transparent copy of page 27 and cover the words *piece* in the second paragraph and *quietly* in the third paragraph. Next, display the transparency and read the passage aloud. As you read, guide students to figure out the covered words. Then reveal the words and point out to students that one way to decipher an unfamiliar word is to leave it out and use the words around it to figure out what would make sense. Follow up by having each student list the strategy on a popcorn- or sardine-shaped cutout and glue the cutout to a construction paper rectangle, making a bookmark reminder to use context clues while reading.

Fact and Opinion

Have each pair of students cut out a copy of the sardine and popcorn patterns at the bottom of this page. Next, guide the twosome to write a statement about the passage from page 27 on each shape and check the appropriate box to show whether the statement is a fact or an opinion. Collect students' work in a bag. Then draw a shape, read its statement, and challenge the class to decide whether it is a fact or an opinion. Repeat as time allows.

Sardines sounds like a fun game.
☐ fact ☑ opinion
Name(s) Jack, Isha

Sticky Popcorn is played in a large space.
☑ fact ☐ opinion
Name(s) Isha, Jack

Making Connections

Have each child draw on a sheet of unlined paper a 3 x 3 grid. Next, guide the student to label it as shown, naming and describing his favorite game in the first column. Then, to compare his favorite game with Sticky Popcorn and Sardines, the child reviews the passage on page 27 and fills in the remaining columns with details about each game.

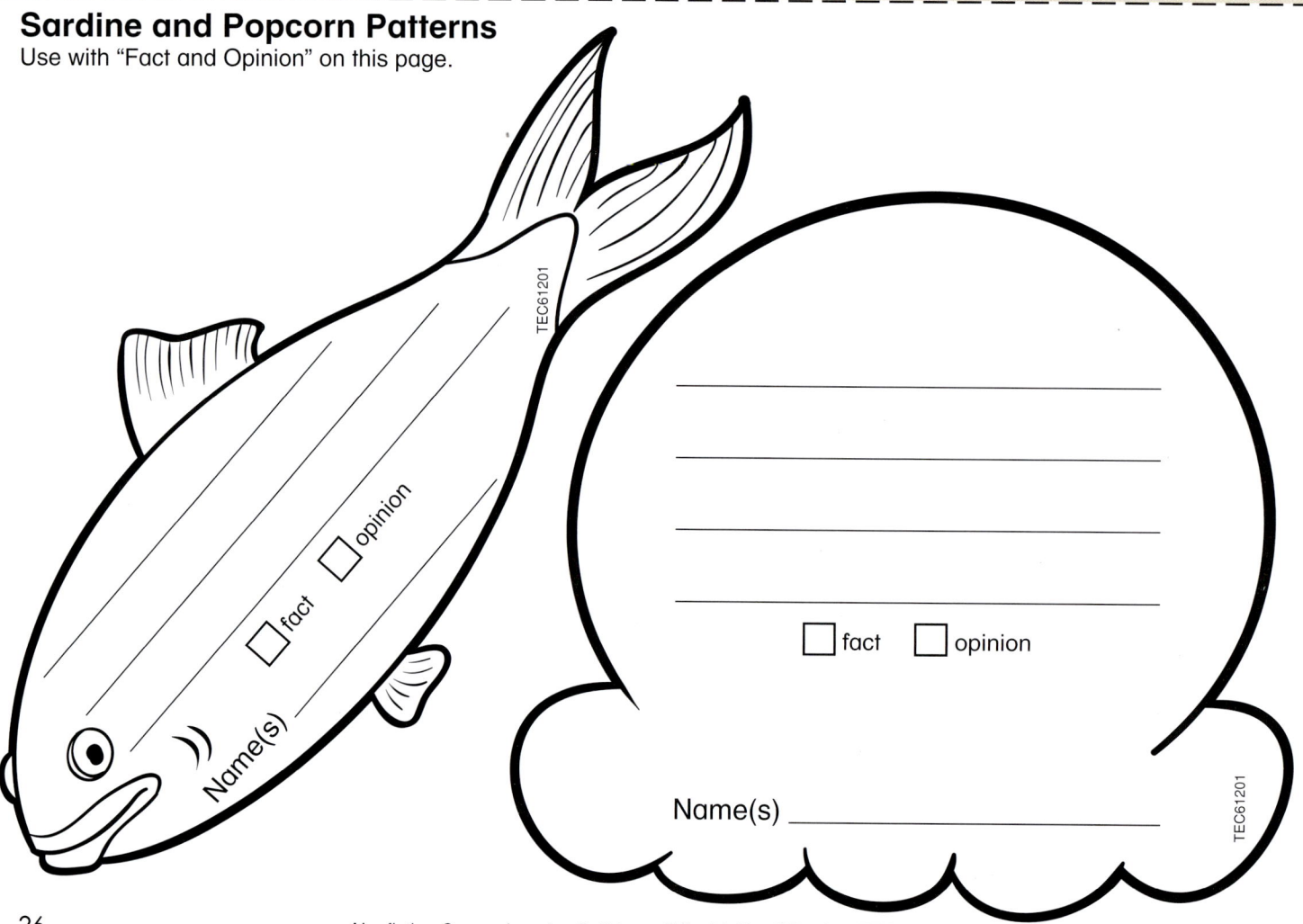

Sardine and Popcorn Patterns
Use with "Fact and Opinion" on this page.

Wacky Games Kids Play

Most kids play games. Some of the games they play are wacky. Sticky Popcorn and Sardines are two wacky games.

Sticky Popcorn is a good game to play in a gym. Each kid acts like a piece of popcorn. He pops around the gym. He looks for other kids, or pieces of popcorn, to stick to. When he finds one, the two kids act as if they are stuck. They pop around together. Then they try to find other kids to stick to them. Kids keep popping around until they all are stuck together.

Sardines is sort of like Hide-and-Seek. One kid is the sardine. The rest of the kids close their eyes while the sardine hides. The group counts to 50. Then each kid looks for the sardine. If someone finds the sardine, she quietly hides with him. Each kid who finds the sardine does the same thing. The kids who are hiding try to stay quiet until only one person is left looking. He becomes the new sardine.

Note to the teacher: Use this reading selection with the activities on pages 25, 26, and 28.

Name_____   Comprehension

Keeping It Wacky!

Circle the letter that shows the best answer to each question.

	Sticky Popcorn	Sardines	Both
1. In which game do kids act like popcorn?	A	L	O
2. Which game can you play with friends?	U	W	S
3. In which game do kids hide?	M	T	P
4. Which game is good to play in a gym?	E	I	Y
5. Which game is wacky?	C	J	G
6. Which game is named after a kind of fish?	N	Z	Q
7. Which game ends when all of the kids are stuck together?	R	B	H
8. In which game do kids count to 50?	K	F	D

What's a great game to play during winter?
To answer the question, write the circled letters from above on the numbered lines below.

___ ___ ___ ___ ___ ___   ___ ___ ___
 8   7   4   4   6   4   3   1   5

Nonfiction Comprehension Builders • ©The Mailbox® Books • TEC61201 • Key p. 110

28   Note to the teacher: Use after reading "Wacky Games Kids Play" on page 27.

"WANTED: FROG FACTS"

with ideas by Kim T. Griswell, Honesdale, PA, and
Colleen Dabney, Williamsburg, VA

EXPLORING TEXT FEATURES

Before reading the selection on page 31, guide students to review a current class reading that is fiction and discuss its text features. Next, give each child a copy of page 31 and help students identify the selection's text features. Then guide students to use a Venn diagram to compare and contrast fiction and nonfiction text features.

Fiction
tells a story
has pictures that help tell the story
has characters
purpose: to entertain

Nonfiction
has headings
has pictures that tell more about the topic
has captions that tell about pictures
gives facts
purpose: to inform

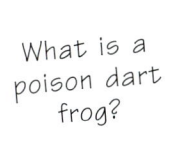

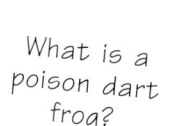

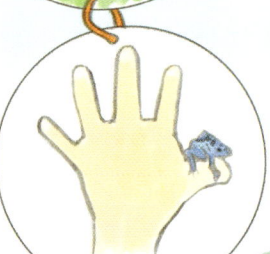

title
pictures

What is a poison dart frog?

Poison dart frogs live in rain forests.

Some are as small as a fingernail.

What is a poison dart frog?

VISUALIZING

Assign each pair of students one sentence from the selection on page 31. Have the duo copy its sentence on one side of a paper plate and then illustrate the sentence on the plate's flip side. Have each pair punch holes in the plate's top and bottom. Then tie the plates together in order and display them near the class library.

CITING TEXT EVIDENCE

To begin, have each pair of students read the summary at the bottom half of this page. Next, guide the pair to reread the selection on page 31 and find words or phrases that support each part of the summary. Have the pair place a transparent counter on each word or phrase that supports the summary. Then have each partner complete a copy of the page below by listing the text evidence where indicated.

Name _____

Citing text evidence

Found: Frog Facts

Find the details that support the summary.

A poison dart frog is a small colorful frog. Its skin has poison that helps keep it safe. Hunters use the poison on their darts.

small	
colorful	
poison	
darts	

Nonfiction Comprehension Builders • ©The Mailbox® Books • TEC61201 • Key p. 110

Note to the teacher: Use with "Citing Text Evidence" on this page.

WANTED: FROG FACTS

What is a poison dart frog?

Poison dart frogs live in rain forests. Some are as small as a fingernail. The biggest poison dart frogs are about three inches long. Their skin may be bright red, orange, green, yellow, or blue. Some poison dart frogs have black spots or bands. Almost all poison dart frogs ooze poison onto their skin. The poison tastes bad and can make animals sick. It helps keep the frogs safe.

How did poison dart frogs get their name?

Hunters in the rain forest use the frogs' poison. Hunters rub their darts on the frogs' skin. Then they use the poison darts to hunt for food.

The blue poison dart frog is blue with black spots.

The strawberry poison dart frog is bright red. It has purple-blue legs.

The green and black poison dart frog may be green or light blue. It has black bands or spots.

Nonfiction Comprehension Builders • ©The Mailbox® Books • TEC61201

Note to the teacher: Have students read each caption and then color each illustration. Use this reading selection with the activities on pages 29, 30, and 32.

Name _____   Letter patterns

Leaping Letters

Cut out each letter card below.
Use the cards to make words.
Record each word on the lines below.

Two-Letter Words

Three-Letter Words

Four-Letter Words

Five-Letter Words

Six-Letter Word

Nonfiction Comprehension Builders • ©The Mailbox® Books • TEC61201

| n | o | p | s | o | i |

32   **Note to the teacher:** Use with "Wanted: Frog Facts" on page 31.

"The Ant-ernet"

by Kim Minafo, Dillard Drive Elementary, Raleigh, NC

talk	touch each other
email	move their antennae
letters	tap on their nests
telephone	squeak
sign language	buzz
cell phone	leave chemical
walkie-talkies	trails
television	
intercom	
books	

Activating Prior Knowledge

To help students focus on ants and how they communicate, draw stick figures showing two people talking and lead students to list ways that we communicate. Next, draw two large ants facing each other and ask students to think about ants and ways that they might communicate. After reading the selection, guide students to review the reading and list ways that ants communicate.

Completing an Outline

After reading the passage aloud, give each pair of students copies of pages 35 and 36. Direct the duo to reread the selection and highlight on page 35 the facts that match each statement on page 36. Next, have the pair cut apart the boxes on its copy of page 36. Then review basic outline structure and guide the twosome to arrange and glue its boxes on the page to complete the outline.

Synonyms

For this center, program six copies of the patterns on page 37 with the vocabulary words and synonyms listed below. Cut out the ant sections and then write a matching letter on the back of each complete set to make the center self-checking. Each student who visits the center reads the words and matches the vocabulary terms with their synonyms. Then each student checks his work and records the words and synonyms in a two-column chart.

Vocabulary Term	Synonyms
talk	speak, tell
movement	motion, stir
warn	alert, alarm
buzz	hum, whir
trail	trace, track
message	word, information

Paraphrasing

To begin, have each child number the paragraphs on a copy of page 35. Next, guide the youngster to stack three 6" x 9" sheets of unlined paper between two 6" x 9" sheets of brown construction paper. Have her staple the pages together and then trim the top half of the stack into an anthill shape and number the pages, front and back. Then the student reads each paragraph and illustrates it on the like-numbered page, leaving space at the bottom for a caption. After illustrating each paragraph, the youngster captions each picture. Finally, she personalizes the cover and shares her paraphrased booklet with a partner.

Ants can't talk. They have other ways to send messages to each other.

ANT

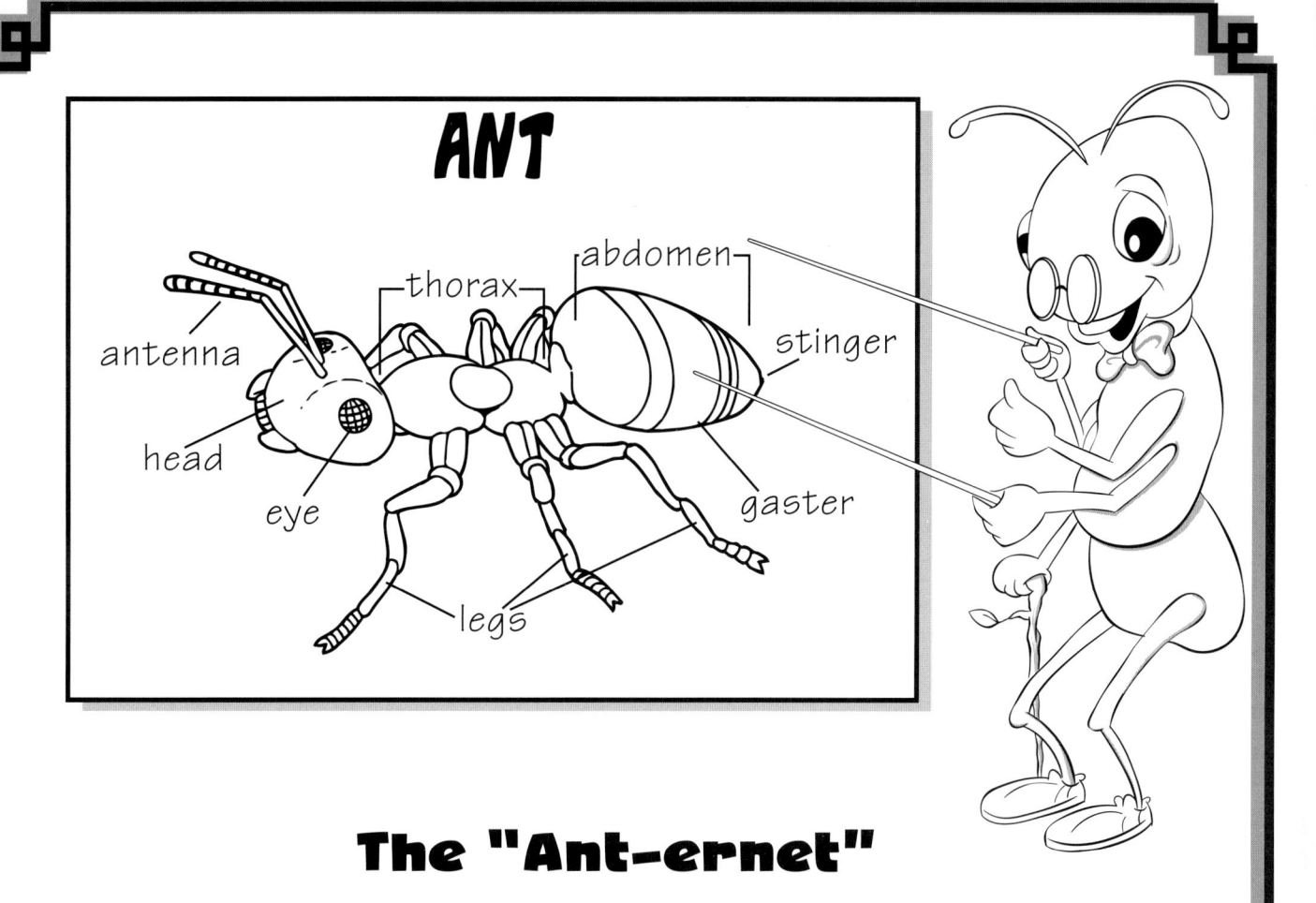

Diagram labels: antenna, head, eye, thorax, abdomen, stinger, gaster, legs

The "Ant-ernet"

Have you ever talked with ants? Of course not! Ants cannot talk, at least not the way we do. But ants do send messages to each other. They use movements, make sounds, and follow chemical trails.

Some ants wiggle their **antennae** to send messages. When two ants meet, they may touch each other's antennae. This can help an ant tell if the other ant is an enemy.

Ants can use sound to send messages. Ants that live in nests inside plants may drum on their homes. To send a message, an ant taps its **gaster** on the nest wall. Each tap sends waves into the nest. The waves can tell other ants about food. The waves can warn other ants about danger.

Some ants even squeak or buzz. The sounds may tell other ants that a nest has caved in. The sounds may tell ants about food or a new nest.

Ants also put down chemical trails that send messages. Ants use many kinds of chemicals. Each chemical has a strong taste or smell that sends a message. Some chemicals tell where to find food. Some chemicals warn ants about danger.

Ants cannot sit down and talk. They cannot send emails or use cell phones. But they keep in touch with movements, sounds, and chemical trails!

Note to the teacher: Use this reading selection with the activities on pages 33, 34, and 36.

Name _____   Completing an outline

Small Talkers

Cut apart each statement.
Glue each one in place to complete the outline.

How Ants Send Messages

I. _____

II. _____

    A. _____

    B. _____

III. _____

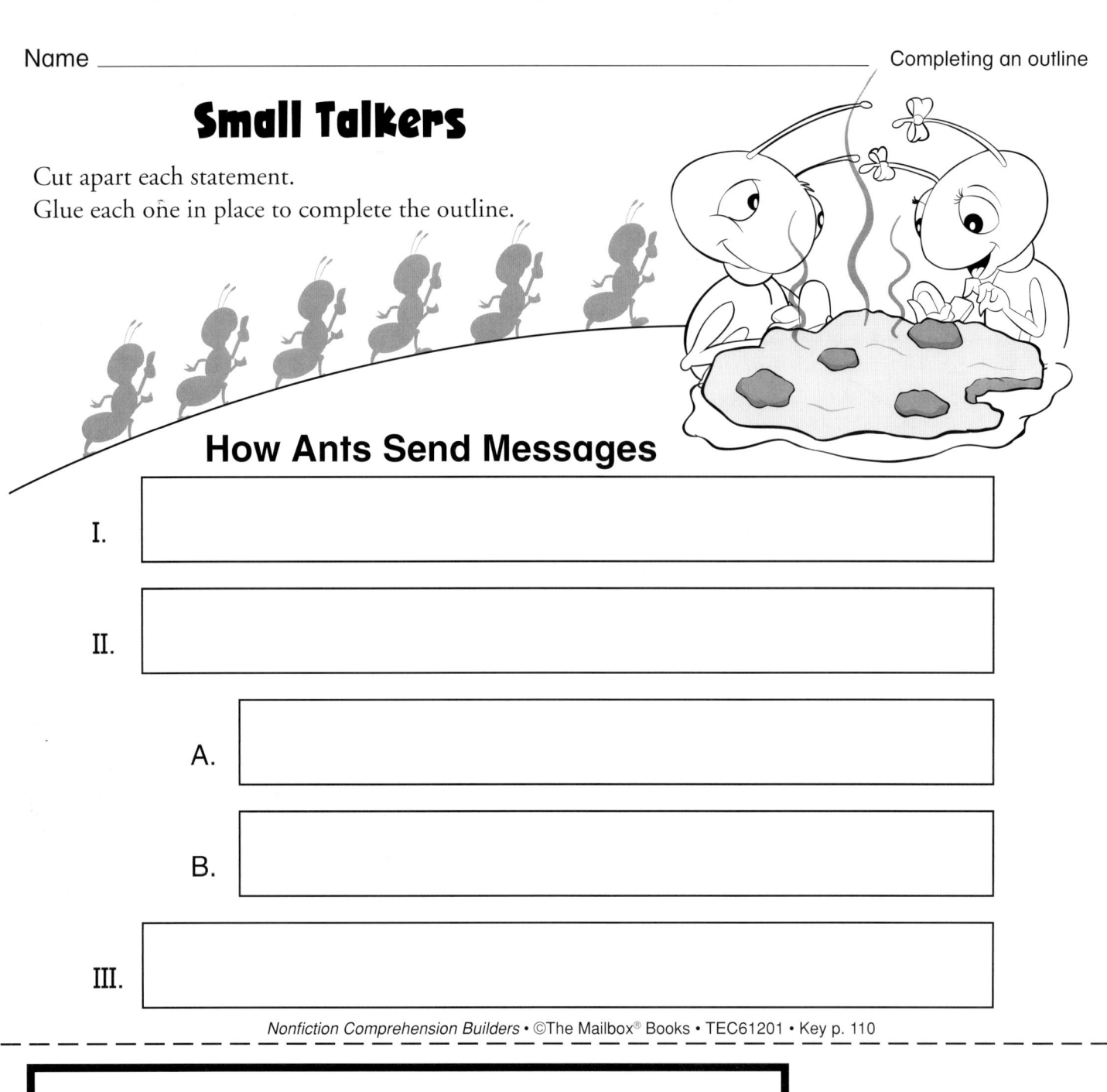

Some ants squeak or buzz.
Some ants tap on nest walls to send messages.
Ants leave chemical trails that send messages.
Ants can wiggle their antennae to send messages.
Ants can use sound to send messages.

Ant Section Patterns
Use with "Synonyms" on page 34.

"HOW TO DRAW A CARTOON CHARACTER"

by Patricia Twohey, Smithfield, RI

ESTABLISHING A PURPOSE FOR READING

Before reading the selection on page 40, lead students to brainstorm a list of how-to examples, such as recipes, craft directions, driving directions, or instructions for playing a game. Next, ask students to think about the best way to read any of those examples. Then guide the class to make a plan for reading how-to materials. (See the example.) Post the plan, give each student a copy of page 40, and direct her to follow the plan to read and follow the directions on the page.

How to Read Directions
1. Read one step at a time.
2. Read the steps in order.
3. Read all of the steps before starting to follow them.

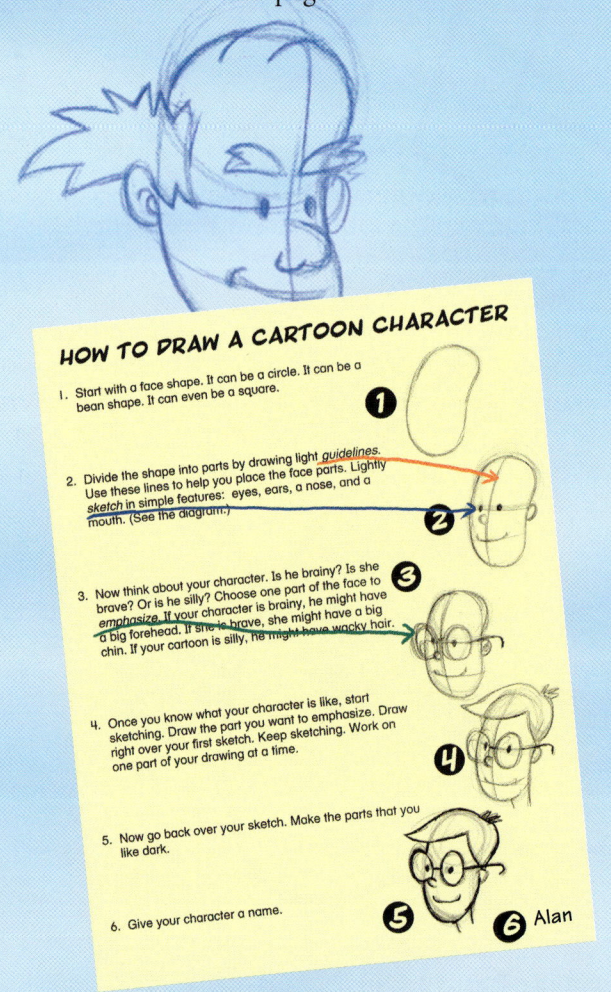

VOCABULARY

To help students better understand the italicized words on page 40, introduce and explain each term before reading. After reading, guide each student to underline each term using a different color and then draw a matching arrow from each underlined word to an illustrated example on the page. Follow up by guiding each child to reread the selection and then list and define each term.

HOW TO DRAW A CARTOON CHARACTER

1. Start with a face shape. It can be a circle. It can be a bean shape. It can even be a square.

2. Divide the shape into parts by drawing light *guidelines*. Use these lines to help you place the face parts. Lightly *sketch* in simple features: eyes, ears, a nose, and a mouth. (See the diagram.)

3. Now think about your character. Is he brainy? Is she brave? Or is he silly? Choose one part of the face to *emphasize*. If your character is brainy, he might have a big forehead. If she is brave, she might have a big chin. If your cartoon is silly, he might have wacky hair.

4. Once you know what your character is like, start sketching. Draw the part you want to emphasize. Draw right over your first sketch. Keep sketching. Work on one part of your drawing at a time.

5. Now go back over your sketch. Make the parts that you like dark.

6. Give your character a name.

Alan

38

FLUENCY

After each student has read and completed the steps on page 40, have him practice reading the selection aloud. When the child can read the page fluently, arrange to have him teach a younger student how to draw a cartoon. For his teaching session, have the student bring the cartoon character he created, a copy of page 40, drawing paper, and a pencil for the younger pupil. Then the student shares his own cartoon character before reading the steps on the page aloud and guiding the youngster to draw a cartoon character of her own.

HOW-TO WRITING

After reading the selection on page 40, have each pair of students study the step-by-step diagrams on a copy of page 41. Next, guide the partners to describe each step using their own words. Then have each student write on a separate sheet of paper six steps that explain how to draw the cartoon character she designed. Have her add diagrams to explain her steps. Bind students' work in a how-to book and place it in your classroom library. It is sure to be a class favorite!

HOW TO DRAW A CARTOON CHARACTER

1. Start with a face shape. It can be a circle. It can be a bean shape. It can even be a square.

2. Divide the shape into parts by drawing light *guidelines*. Use these lines to help you place the face parts. Lightly *sketch* in simple features: eyes, ears, a nose, and a mouth. (See the diagram.)

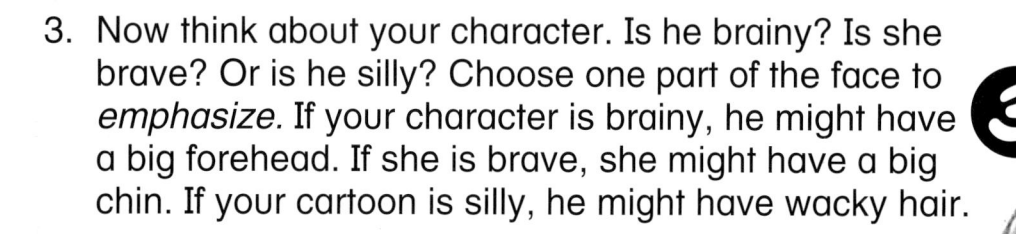

3. Now think about your character. Is he brainy? Is she brave? Or is he silly? Choose one part of the face to *emphasize*. If your character is brainy, he might have a big forehead. If she is brave, she might have a big chin. If your cartoon is silly, he might have wacky hair.

4. Once you know what your character is like, start sketching. Draw the part you want to emphasize. Draw right over your first sketch. Keep sketching. Work on one part of your drawing at a time.

5. Now go back over your sketch. Make the parts that you like dark.

6. Give your character a name.

Name _____   Paraphrasing

Step-by-Step

Study the diagrams.
Use your own words to explain each one.

1. _____ _____ _____ _____ _____	2. _____ _____ _____ _____ _____
3. _____ _____ _____ _____ _____	4. _____ _____ _____ _____ _____
5. _____ _____ _____ _____ _____	6. _____ _____ _____ _____ _____ Alan

Nonfiction Comprehension Builders • ©The Mailbox® Books • TEC61201 • Key p. 110

Note to the teacher: Use with "How-to Writing" on page 39.

41

"Pouch Potatoes"

Making and Confirming Predictions

Before reading the selection on page 44, guide each student to complete the "Before Reading" and "Why You Think That" sections on a copy of page 45. Next, have the child read the selection and then reread the statements on his copy of page 45 and complete the "After Reading" section. To follow up, lead small groups of students to discuss their answers.

Vocabulary

To explore the selection's vocabulary, have each student pair cut apart the cards on a copy of the bottom of page 43. Then guide each duo to use the cards to play a memory game, matching each word with its illustration. The winner is the student with more matches. To follow up, have the pair read a copy of the selection on page 44 and highlight each vocabulary term.

Summarizing

After each child reads a copy of the selection on page 44, have him highlight each question and its answer. Next, guide the child to paraphrase the answer in one sentence. Then have the child put her four sentences together in a one-paragraph selection summary.

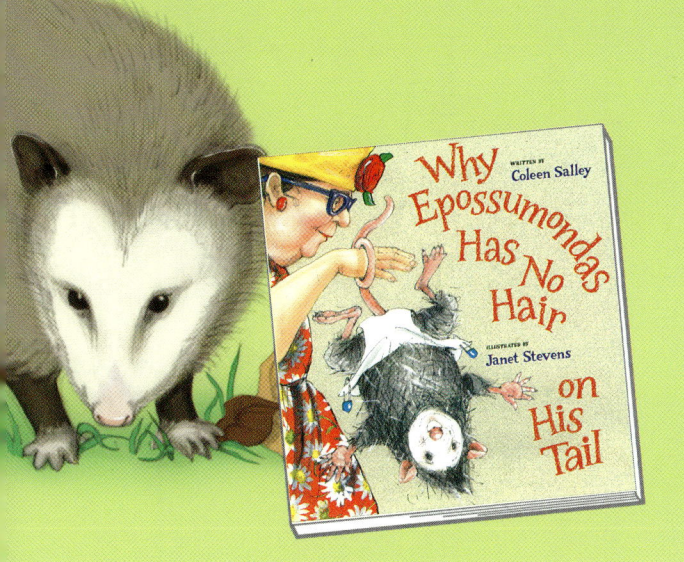

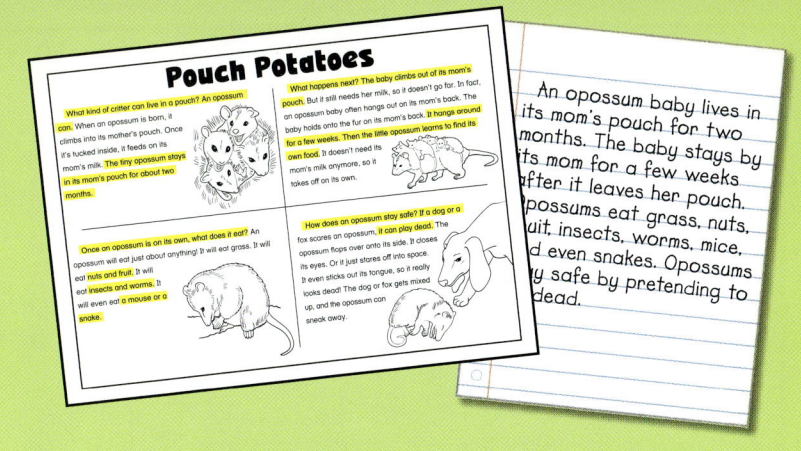

Connecting Fiction and Nonfiction

After reading the selection on page 44, read aloud *Why Epossumondas Has No Hair on His Tail* by Coleen Salley. Then guide each pair of students to write and illustrate a folktale that explains why opossum babies crawl into their mothers' pouches, why opossum babies ride around on their mothers' backs, why opossums eat grass and worms, or why opossums play dead. Have each pair share its story and then bind students' work in a class book that's sure to be read over and over again!

Vocabulary Cards
Use with "Vocabulary" on page 42.

opossum	climbs	stares	learns
TEC61201	TEC61201	TEC61201	TEC61201

holds	flops		
TEC61201	TEC61201	TEC61201	TEC61201

TEC61201	TEC61201	TEC61201	TEC61201

Nonfiction Comprehension Builders • ©The Mailbox® Books • TEC61201

Pouch Potatoes

What kind of critter can live in a pouch? An opossum can. When an opossum is born, it climbs into its mother's pouch. Once it's tucked inside, it feeds on its mom's milk. The tiny opossum stays in its mom's pouch for about two months.

What happens next? The baby climbs out of its mom's pouch. But it still needs her milk, so it doesn't go far. In fact, an opossum baby often hangs out on its mom's back. The baby holds onto the fur on its mom's back. It hangs around for a few weeks. Then the little opossum learns to find its own food. It doesn't need its mom's milk anymore, so it takes off on its own.

Once an opossum is on its own, what does it eat? An opossum will eat just about anything! It will eat grass. It will eat nuts and fruit. It will eat insects and worms. It will even eat a mouse or a snake.

How does an opossum stay safe? If a dog or a fox scares an opossum, it can play dead. The opossum flops over onto its side. It closes its eyes. Or it just stares off into space. It even sticks out its tongue, so it really looks dead! The dog or fox gets mixed up, and the opossum can sneak away.

Nonfiction Comprehension Builders • ©The Mailbox® Books • TEC61201

Note to the teacher: Use with the activities on pages 42, 43, and 45.

Name _____

Anticipation guide

Possum Particulars

Read each statement.
Color the number that shows what you think.
Then tell why you think that.

1 = It's a fact.
2 = It's probably a fact.
3 = It's probably not a fact.
4 = It's not a fact.

	Before Reading	Why You Think That	After Reading
1. Some opossum babies live in their moms' pouches.	1 2 3 4		1 2 3 4
2. Opossums don't ride on their moms' backs.	1 2 3 4		1 2 3 4
3. Opossums eat only meat.	1 2 3 4		1 2 3 4
4. When an opossum gets scared, it can play dead.	1 2 3 4		1 2 3 4

Nonfiction Comprehension Builders • ©The Mailbox® Books • TEC61201

Note to the teacher: Use with "Making and Confirming Predictions" on page 42.

45

"ON THE RECORD: VIDEO GAMES"

by Starin Lewis, Phoenix, AZ

VOCABULARY

Before reading the selection on page 48, list several vocabulary words as shown. Next, lead students to share what they already know and what they notice about each word, such as syllable breaks, word parts they recognize, roots, affixes, and predicted meanings. Then read the passage aloud, pointing out each listed word. After reading, have students review each list and add new observations and ideas. Finally, guide students to look up each word, read its definition, and use the list to paraphrase its meaning.

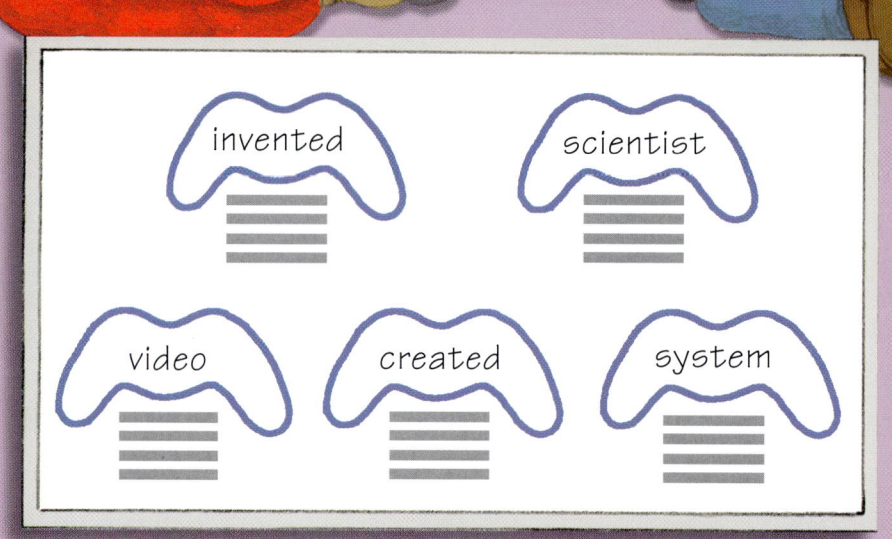

invented • scientist • video • created • system

text
"A big change came in 1972. That was the first year you could buy a video game system to play at home."

text-to-self connection
It made me think about my dad's old video game. We play it together sometimes. The graphics are really plain, but the games are fun.

MAKING CONNECTIONS

Have each child fold an index card in half and label one side "text." Next, direct him to reread the passage on page 48. As he reads, have him jot down on the card's labeled side a sentence or two that helps him make a text-to-self, text-to-text, or text-to-world connection. Then have him flip the card, list the type of connection, and write about it. To share their connections, have students display their cards on their desks. Set aside a few minutes and guide students to stroll around the room, reading about their classmates' connections.

SUMMARIZING

Copy the handheld video game pattern and strip at the bottom of this page for each student. Next, guide the child to summarize in each space on the strip the selection's three main events. Have her slide the strip through the handheld video game, as shown, and take her summarized video game history home to share.

MAIN IDEA AND SUPPORTING DETAILS

Have each child identify the passage's main idea and list it in the first section on a copy of the strip from the bottom of this page. Next, guide him to list two supporting details on the remaining sections and slide the strip through the slits on a copy of the handheld video game as shown. Then have each student share his work with a partner.

Handheld Video Game Pattern and Strip
Use with "Summarizing" and "Main Idea and Supporting Details" on this page.

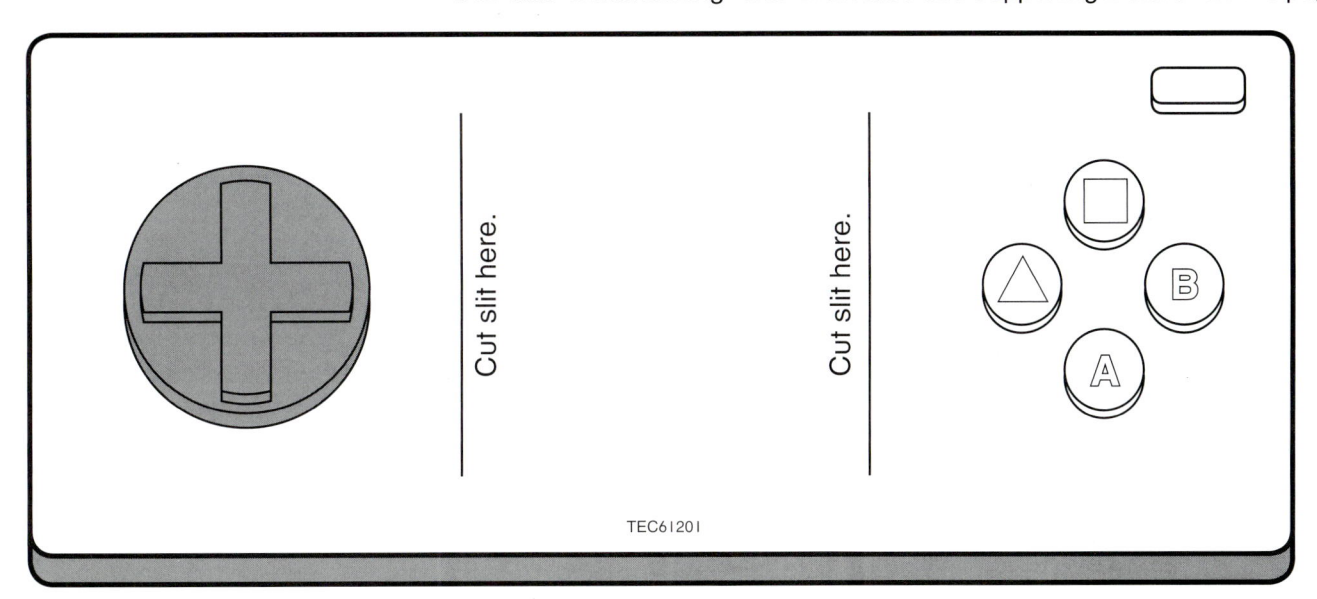

Cut slit here.

Cut slit here.

TEC61201

Nonfiction Comprehension Builders • ©The Mailbox® Books • TEC61201

ON THE RECORD: VIDEO GAMES

The first known computer game was invented in 1952. It was a game of tic-tac-toe. That may sound simple. But to play this game, you had to have a computer that took up a whole room.

In 1958, a scientist wanted people to enjoy their visit to his lab's open house. But he also wanted to show off the lab's work. So he created the game *Tennis for Two.* People loved it. They lined up outside the lab to play. *Tennis for Two* was a success at the next open house too. Then the game was taken apart, and its parts were used for other projects.

A big change came in 1972. That was the first year you could buy a video game system to play at home. The Odyssey system cost about $100. You hooked it up to your TV, and you could play 12 different games. The game system was a hit! People loved being able to play a video game at home.

In the last 50 years, video games have really changed! The systems are smaller. The games are much more involved. The graphics seem real. It makes you wonder what video games will be like after the next 50 years.

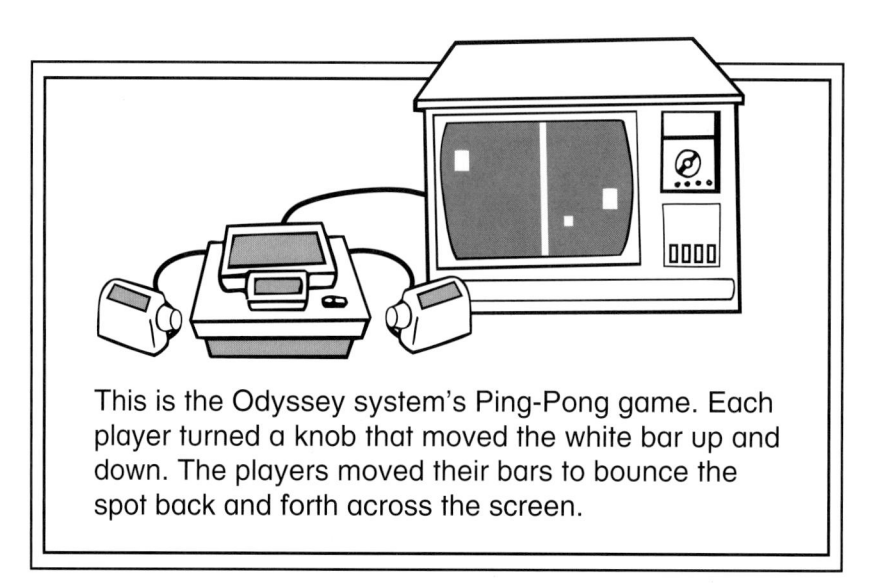

The first computer game was simple, but it needed a huge computer.

No one kept score when they played *Tennis for Two.*

This is the Odyssey system's Ping-Pong game. Each player turned a knob that moved the white bar up and down. The players moved their bars to bounce the spot back and forth across the screen.

Name _____   Comprehension

Your Play

Shade the correct answer.

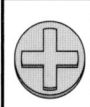

1. Which event came first?

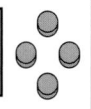

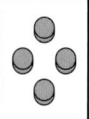

- (N) Parts from *Tennis for Two* were used for other projects.
- (A) The Odyssey home video game system was made.
- (I) A tic-tac-toe computer game was invented.
- (D) The video game *Tennis for Two* was invented.

2. What is the selection mostly about?

- (S) the history of video games
- (T) how much video games cost
- (B) playing video games
- (G) how much people like to play video games

3. Which of these is an opinion?

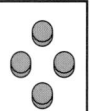

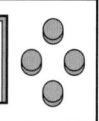

- (F) Video games have really changed since 1952.
- (H) Video games are a lot more fun than they were in 1972.
- (E) The first home video game cost about $100.
- (M) To play the first video game, you had to have a huge computer.

4. Why was the game *Tennis for Two* taken apart?

- (O) No one liked to play *Tennis for Two*.
- (W) You needed a huge computer to play *Tennis for Two*.
- (J) There were too many other games to play.
- (P) The game's parts were used for other projects.

5. Which of these is a fact from the selection?

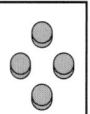

- (K) Many people think video games are harmful.
- (U) The inventor of *Tennis for Two* should have sold the game.
- (C) Before 1972, you could not buy a home video game system.
- (R) Video games may all be 3-D in the future.

What is a computer's favorite snack?
To find out, write each shaded letter on the matching numbered line below.

___ ___ ___ ___ ___ !
 5   3   1   4   2

Nonfiction Comprehension Builders • ©The Mailbox® Books • TEC61201 • Key p. 110

Note to the teacher: Use with "On the Record: Video Games" on page 48.

49

"Just for Luck!"

*reading selection by Kim T. Griswell, Honesdale, PA
with ideas by Carol Felts, Rensselaer, NY*

Context Clues

Put the focus on context clues by giving each student three colored pencils and a copy of the passage on page 52. Guide each student to circle with one color the word *athletes*. Lead the child to also circle *sports stars* and *players* and point out that the words' meanings are similar. Next, have each student circle with another color the word *routines* and guide students to identify and circle the phrase that defines it *(do the exact same things on each game day)* with the same color. Guide students to circle with the third color the word *trinkets* and then look for and circle words or phrases that tell what that word means *(coins, four-leaf clovers, or other small objects)*. Then guide students to read the passage, referring to their circled clues to verify the words' meanings each time they appear.

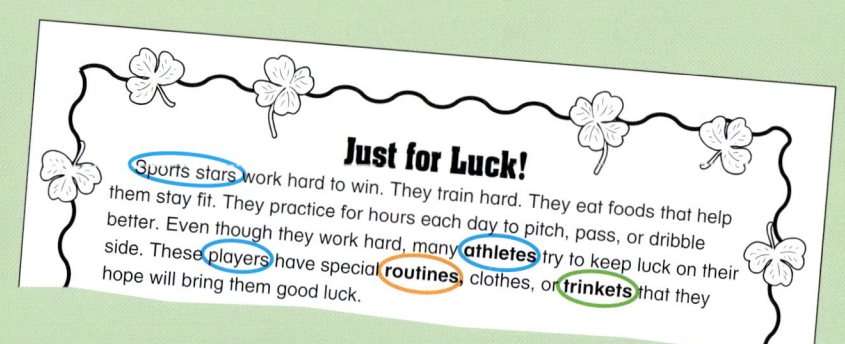

Just for Luck!

Sports stars work hard to win. They train hard. They eat foods that help them stay fit. They practice for hours each day to pitch, pass, or dribble better. Even though they work hard, many athletes try to keep luck on their side. These players have special routines, clothes, or trinkets that they hope will bring them good luck.

Visualizing

Help students better understand the passage by drawing on what they know and what they read. Give each small group of students a 3' x 3' piece of bulletin board paper and a copy of page 52. Direct the group to reread the passage and then create a mural that illustrates it. As each group shares its finished work, have the students identify the text from the passage that inspired it. Then display students' murals along with copies of the passage under the title "Read It. See It!"

Identifying Important Details

For this award-winning idea, copy page 52 and the medal cards on this page for each student. Have the child cut apart and color the cards. Next, read aloud each sentence from the passage. Guide each student to hold up the medal that shows the detail's significance: gold (very important), silver (important), or bronze (interesting but not important). Direct children to highlight each detail that the class determines is very important. Then have each student use the highlighted details to summarize the passage.

Special routines help some players feel lucky.

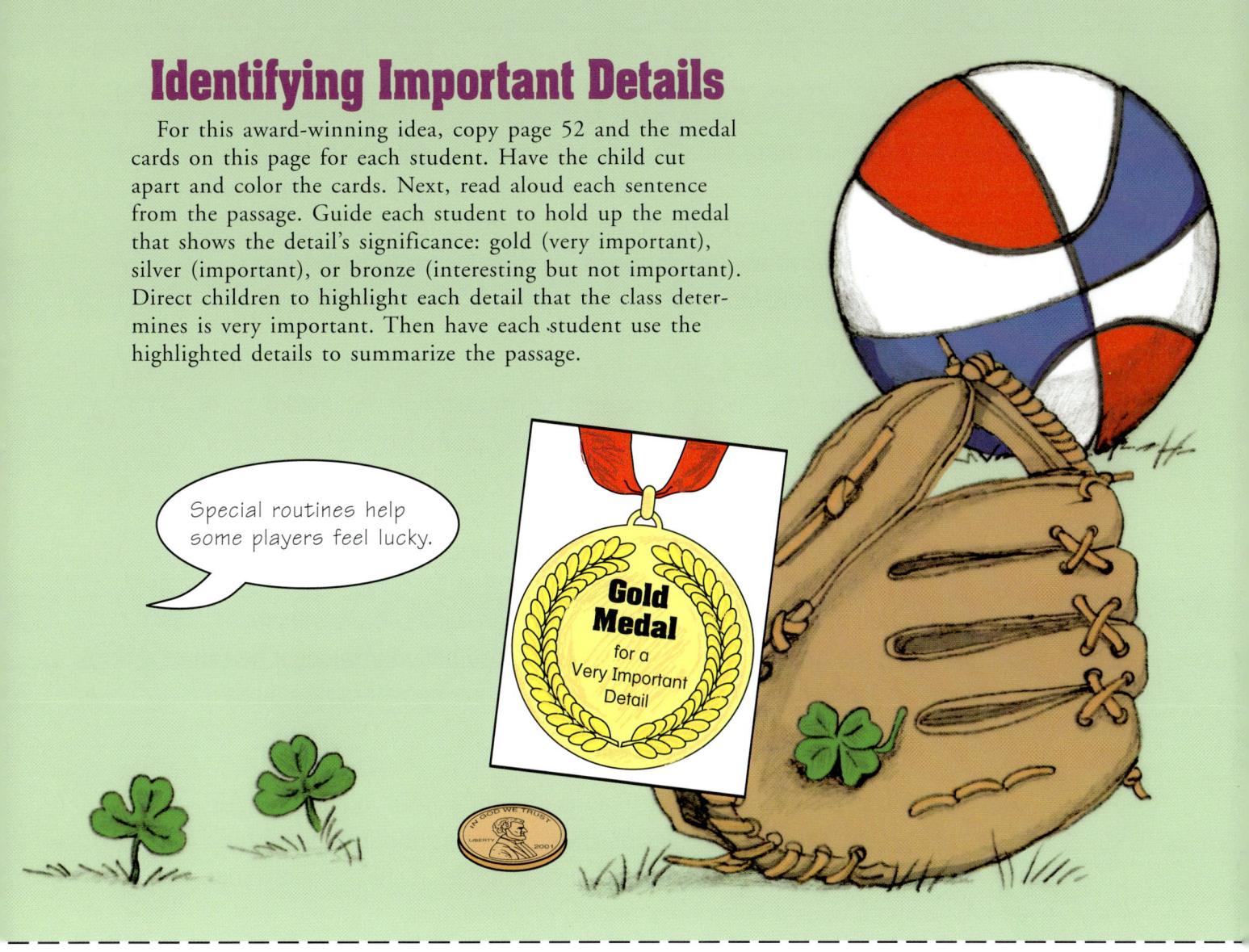

Medal Cards
Use with "Identifying Important Details" on this page.

Gold Medal for a Very Important Detail

Silver Medal for an Important Detail

Bronze Medal for an Interesting Detail That Is Not Important

TEC61201

Nonfiction Comprehension Builders • ©The Mailbox® Books • TEC61201

Just for Luck!

Sports stars work hard to win. They train hard. They eat foods that help them stay fit. They practice for hours each day to pitch, pass, or dribble better. Even though they work hard, many **athletes** try to keep luck on their side. These players have special **routines,** clothes, or **trinkets** that they hope will bring them good luck.

Special routines help some players feel lucky. They do the exact same things on each game day. For one baseball player, working crossword puzzles before he played seemed lucky. A hockey star always tucked in his jersey on the right side. The linebackers on one football team all got dressed an hour before each game; then they sat together in the stands. Many basketball players wipe the soles of their shoes for luck.

For some sports stars, clothes are the key. There was a baseball player who wore the same undershirt for six years. One football star felt as if he ran faster when he wore white shoes. If his team lost, one soccer player threw away his socks.

Many athletes carry or wear lucky trinkets like coins, four-leaf clovers, or other small objects. One basketball star always wore a rubber band on his right wrist. A tennis star always wore the same earrings. One baseball player even kept a sugar packet in his back pocket for good luck.

Many sports stars never stop working hard. But many athletes also hope for good luck when they play. Those players have routines, clothes, or objects that help them feel lucky.

Name _____

Comprehension

Looking for Luck

Shade the correct answer below.

1. In the first paragraph, another word used for *sports stars* is
   - ⓝ fans
   - ⓕ trainers
   - ⓣ athletes

2. What is the main idea of the passage?
   - ⓤ Even though they work hard, many sports stars hope for good luck.
   - ⓑ Sports stars always wear the same undershirts.
   - ⓙ Many basketball players wipe the soles of their shoes for luck.

3. Which of these is a fact from the passage?
   - ⓙ You will run faster if you wear white shoes.
   - ⓘ Many athletes carry lucky trinkets.
   - ⓥ Rubber bands bring good luck.

4. In this passage, what does *routine* mean?
   - ⓗ special trinkets
   - ⓩ lucky clothes
   - ⓔ something you always do the exact same way

5. Which of the following is an opinion?
   - ⓒ Sports stars eat foods that help them stay fit.
   - ⓟ Wearing the same earrings every time you play tennis is lucky.
   - ⓠ Most athletes practice for hours each day.

6. Which of the following trinkets are listed in the passage?
   - ⓦ coins
   - ⓨ earrings
   - ⓞ both coins and earrings

7. One soccer player always
   - ⓒ wore the same undershirt
   - ⓡ threw away his socks if his team lost
   - ⓓ wore white shoes

8. Why did the author write this selection?
   - ⓢ to tell about things sports stars do for good luck
   - ⓙ to tell about a famous baseball player
   - ⓥ to tell how to be a famous sports star

If someone always follows a game-day routine, you might say that person is _____.
To find out, write each shaded letter on the numbered line below.

___ ___ ___ ___ ___ ___ ___ ___ ___ ___ ___ ___
 8   2   5   4   7   8   1   3   1   3   6   2   8

Note to the teacher: Use with "Just for Luck!" on page 52.

53

"Jon Scieszka"

Say Shes-ka

by Amy Satkoski, Orchard Park Elementary
Carmel, IN

Vocabulary

Before reading the selection on page 56, divide students into three groups. Assign each group a bold word from the selection. Direct the group to come up with an easy-to-understand definition for the word and record it on a large sheet of paper. Also have the group add drawings to help students understand and remember what the word means. Next, give each child a copy of page 56 and have him record his group's definition in the appropriate box on the page. Then have each group present its word and definition while the remaining students record the meaning in its appropriate box.

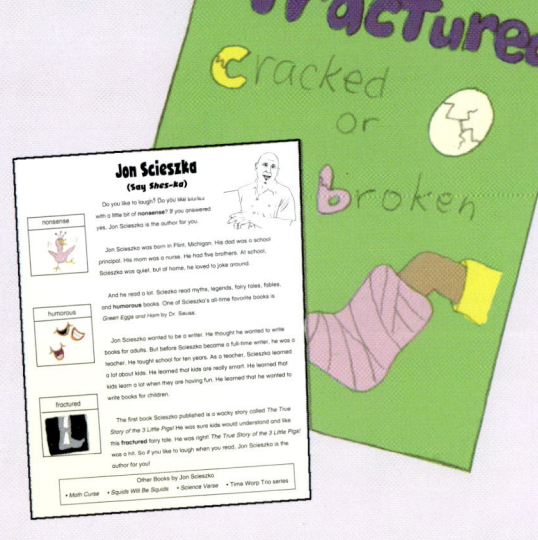

If you answered yes, Jon S. is the author for you.

Reading Proper Names

Point out to students Jon Scieszka's name and its pronunciation in the title of the selection. Next, lead students to repeat the name with you. Then guide each child to point to Scieszka's name in the first and second paragraphs and read it aloud with you. Then, before students read the selection independently, remind them that when they come to a hard-to-read proper name such as Scieszka's, they can substitute an initial for the hard-to-read name and keep reading.

54

Questioning

After reading the selection on page 56, guide each child to write on a large sticky note a question about her reading. Next, have the student post her question on the board and then write another question. After a set amount of time, have each child return to the board and take another student's question. She reads the question and then flips the note to record her answer. She returns the sticky note to the board and takes another one as time allows. When all the questions have been answered, each child collects her notes and reviews the answers. If desired, post a copy of page 56 along with students' notes on a display titled "Ask Questions While You Read!"

Critical Thinking

For this group activity, post the questions shown on separate sheets of chart paper and divide the class into small groups. Then guide each group to choose a question and answer it following the steps shown. If desired, use a timer to help students stay on schedule. After each group has answered all of the questions, unfold the charts and lead students to discuss them.

Steps:
1. Read the question and skim the selection to find the answer. (two minutes)
2. Discuss the question and its best answer with your group. (four minutes)
3. Write your group's answer on the bottom of the chart and then fold the chart so that it covers your answer. (one minute)
4. Repeat Steps 1–3 for the next question.

JON SCIESZKA
(SAY SHES-KA)

Do you like to laugh? Do you like stories with a little bit of **nonsense**? If you answered yes, Jon Scieszka is the author for you.

nonsense

Jon Scieszka was born in Flint, Michigan. His dad was a school principal. His mom was a nurse. He had five brothers. At school, Scieszka was quiet, but at home, he loved to joke around.

And he read a lot. Sciezka read myths, legends, fairy tales, fables, and **humorous** books. One of Scieszka's all-time favorite books is *Green Eggs and Ham* by Dr. Seuss.

humorous

Jon Scieszka wanted to be a writer. He thought he wanted to write books for adults. But before Scieszka became a full-time writer, he was a teacher. He taught school for ten years. As a teacher, Scieszka learned a lot about kids. He learned that kids are really smart. He learned that kids learn a lot when they are having fun. He learned that he wanted to write books for children.

fractured

The first book Scieszka published is a wacky story called *The True Story of the 3 Little Pigs!* He was sure kids would understand and like this **fractured** fairy tale. He was right! *The True Story of the 3 Little Pigs!* was a hit. So if you like to laugh when you read, Jon Scieszka is the author for you!

Other Books by Jon Scieszka

• *Math Curse* • *Squids Will Be Squids* • *Science Verse* • *Time Warp Trio* series

---

Note to the teacher: Use this reading selection with the activities on pages 54, 55, and 57.

Name _____ Finding answers in text

Pencil Check

Number each paragraph in "Jon Scieszka (Say *Shes-ka*)."
If the statement is true, color the eraser.
Then write the number of the paragraph that helped you choose.
The first one has been done for you.

- Jon Scieszka was born in Michigan. **2**
- Scieszka liked to joke around at school.
- Scieszka's first book was *The Stinky Cheese Man and Other Fairly Stupid Tales.*
- Scieszka wanted to be a writer.
- Scieszka never read myths or legends.
- Scieszka had four brothers.
- Scieszka's first book was a hit.
- Scieszka was a schoolteacher for ten years.

Nonfiction Comprehension Builders • ©The Mailbox® Books • TEC61201 • Key p. 110

Note to the teacher: Use with "Jon Scieszka (Say *Shes-ka*)" on page 56.

"Shark Sense"

by Angela Rood, Dyersburg Intermediate School, Dyersburg, TN

Activating Prior Knowledge

Before students dive into the passage, copy page 61 for each pair of students. Have the duo fold under the right side of the page and then complete each sentence starter to share what they already know about sharks. Next, read aloud each sentence beginning and have volunteers share their endings. Read the passage aloud as students read along silently. Then guide each twosome to unfold the right side of page 61 and follow the directions to complete each shark fact.

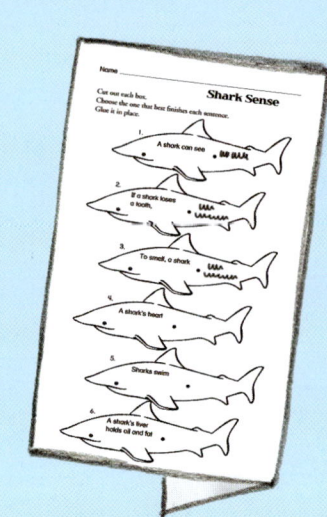

Main Idea

Point out to students that in nonfiction text, a paragraph's first sentence often tells its main idea. Guide each student to number the passage's paragraphs on a copy of page 60 and then highlight the first sentences in paragraphs 2, 3, 4, and 5. Next, have the youngster make four cutouts that resemble a shark's dorsal fin. Direct him to reread each paragraph, copy its highlighted sentence onto one of the fin shapes, and then illustrate the main idea, showing supporting details from the paragraph. Have students staple their pages together, as shown, before they share their work and explain how their illustrations support their topic sentence.

Fact and Opinion

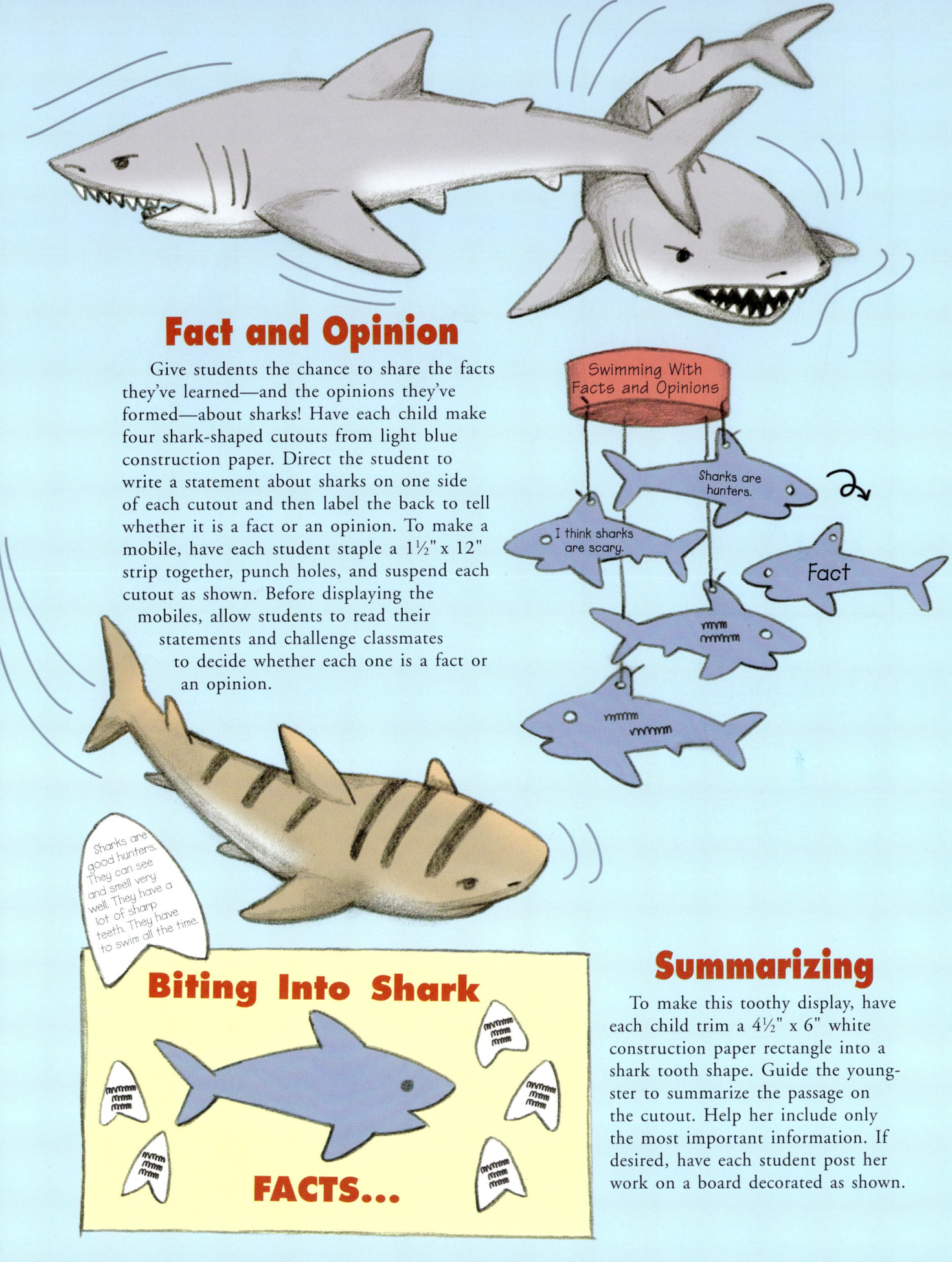

Give students the chance to share the facts they've learned—and the opinions they've formed—about sharks! Have each child make four shark-shaped cutouts from light blue construction paper. Direct the student to write a statement about sharks on one side of each cutout and then label the back to tell whether it is a fact or an opinion. To make a mobile, have each student staple a 1½" x 12" strip together, punch holes, and suspend each cutout as shown. Before displaying the mobiles, allow students to read their statements and challenge classmates to decide whether each one is a fact or an opinion.

Summarizing

To make this toothy display, have each child trim a 4½" x 6" white construction paper rectangle into a shark tooth shape. Guide the youngster to summarize the passage on the cutout. Help her include only the most important information. If desired, have each student post her work on a board decorated as shown.

Shark Sense

On a hot summer day, what could keep people out of the cool ocean waves? The sight of a shark swimming by might scare people away. But there is more to sharks than their scary looks!

Sharks are hunters with sharp senses. Sharks have keen sight. They can see very well, even in dark water. A shark's sense of smell is strong too. It uses almost one-third of its brain just for smelling.

Sharks are famous for their sharp teeth. Some sharks have two rows of front teeth. Others have eight! A shark grows new teeth to replace the ones it loses. A shark may have as many as 30,000 teeth in its lifetime!

Swimming sharks may look as if they are hunting. But most sharks need to swim all of the time. A shark's large liver stores oil and fat. Oil and fat are lighter than water and help the shark float. Still, a shark has to keep swimming, or it will sink.

For some sharks, swimming also keeps their blood pumping. A shark's heart is very small. Swimming moves muscles that keep the shark's blood moving.

Sharks have keen senses and sharp teeth, and most move all the time. If you spot one, will you stay on the beach?

Name _____   Activating prior knowledge

Shark Sense

Cut out each box.
Choose the one that best finishes each sentence.
Glue it in place.

1. A shark can see

2. If a shark loses a tooth,

3. To smell, a shark

4. A shark's heart

5. Sharks swim

6. A shark's liver holds oil and fat

- that help the shark float.

- uses almost one-third of its brain.

- very well in dark water.

- is very small.

- it grows a new tooth to replace it.

- most of the time to keep from sinking.

Nonfiction Comprehension Builders • ©The Mailbox® Books • TEC61201 • Key p. 111

Note to the teacher: Use with "Activating Prior Knowledge" on page 58.

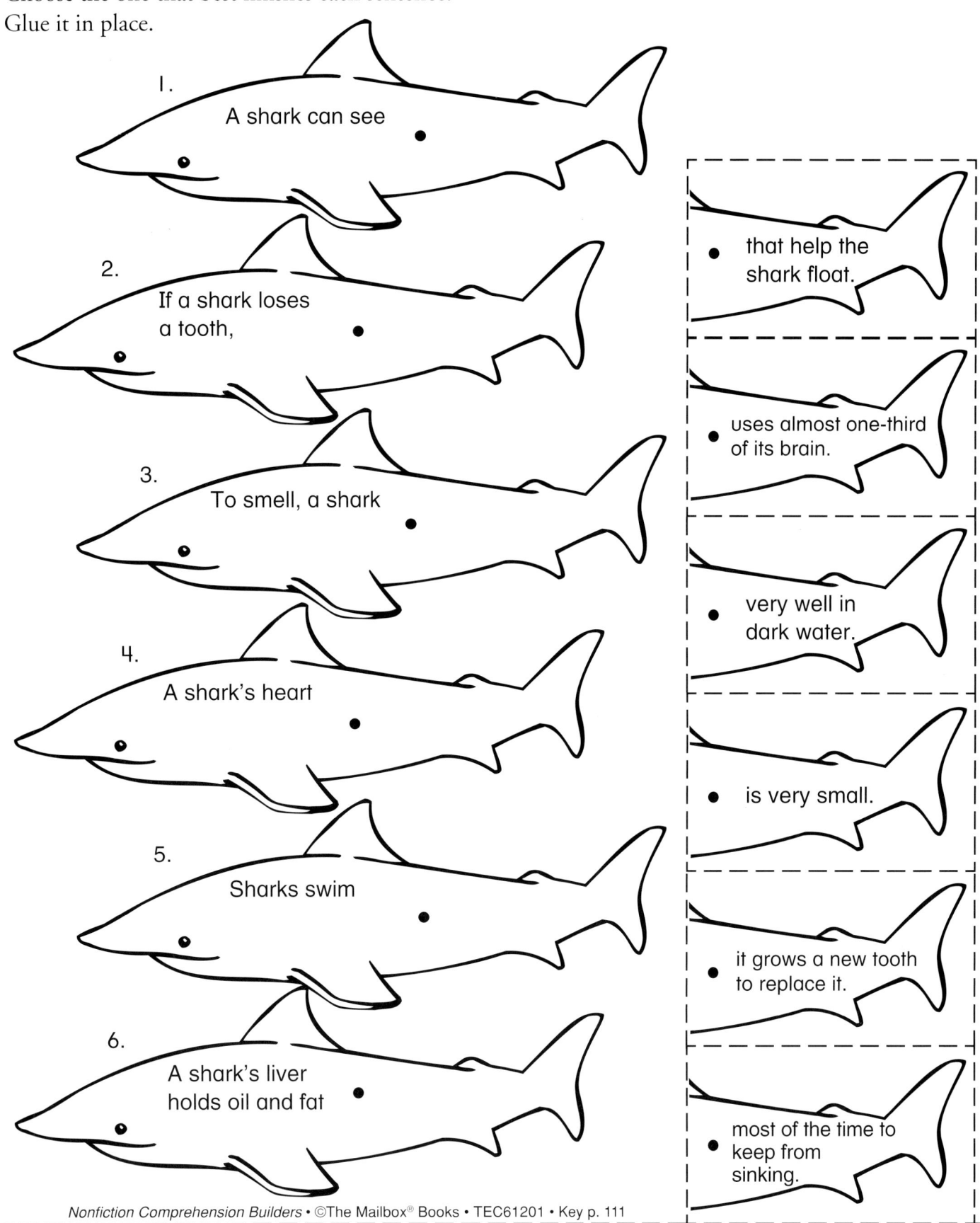

"Eating Machines"

by S. E. H. Riddle, Dorchester, MA

VOCABULARY

Create six piranhas for this engaging prereading center by cutting small triangles out of 12 paper plates. Staple each pair of plates together, use the cutout triangles to make the tail, and add piranha details as shown. Next, copy and cut out the cards on page 65. Glue one definition to each piranha and then place each fish card in a small container along with shredded blue and green paper. Guide each student at the center to read each definition and hunt for its matching term. The child drops each fish card inside the matching piranha's mouth. Then, in a three-column chart, she records each term, its definition, and an illustration.

QUESTIONING

For this student-created game, guide each pair of students to read the selection on page 64 and write five questions on index cards as they read. Have the pair also list the answer on each card and then decorate the flip side to look like a piranha. Next, instruct each pair of students to work with another pair to create a lake mat on a large sheet of construction paper. Then have both pairs place their cards piranha side up on the mat.

To play, Player 1 tosses a marker onto the lake mat. Player 2 takes the card nearest the marker and reads aloud the question. Player 1 answers the question, referring to the reading selection as necessary. If Player 1 answers correctly, Player 2 gives him the card. If Player 1 is incorrect, Player 2 returns the card to the lake. The remaining players take turns in the same manner. After a set amount of time, the student with the most cards is declared the winner.

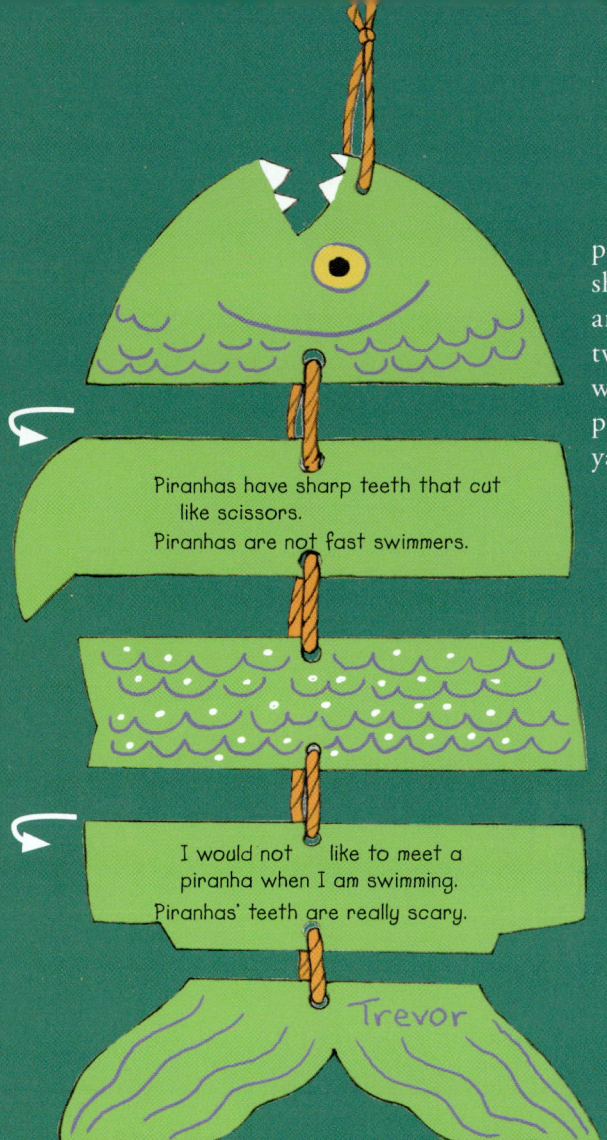

FACT AND OPINION

Have each student create a piranha-shaped construction paper cutout and then cut the shape into five sections as shown. Direct the child to record his name on the tail section and then list two facts from the selection on the cutout's first two sections. In the remaining sections, guide the student to write two opinion statements about piranhas. Have the child punch holes in each section and tie the pieces together with yarn. Then hang the finished projects to display them.

Piranhas have sharp teeth that cut like scissors.
Piranhas are not fast swimmers.

I would not like to meet a piranha when I am swimming.
Piranhas' teeth are really scary.

Trevor

POINT OF VIEW

Follow the steps below to make a point of view finder. Next, have each pair of students spin the finder. Guide the partners to describe a piranha from a small fish's, frog's, human's, or piranha's point of view, depending on the spin. To have students share their work, spin the point of view finder and call on a pair of students to share its description from that point of view.

Materials: 2 paper plates, cardboard tube, brass fastener, scissors

Steps:
1. Cut off the ruffled edge of one paper plate.
2. Cut a hole the diameter of the cardboard tube near the plate's edge. Insert the cardboard tube.
3. Turn the other paper plate over and divide the center section into fourths. Label each section as shown.
4. Loosely connect the two plates using the brass fastener.

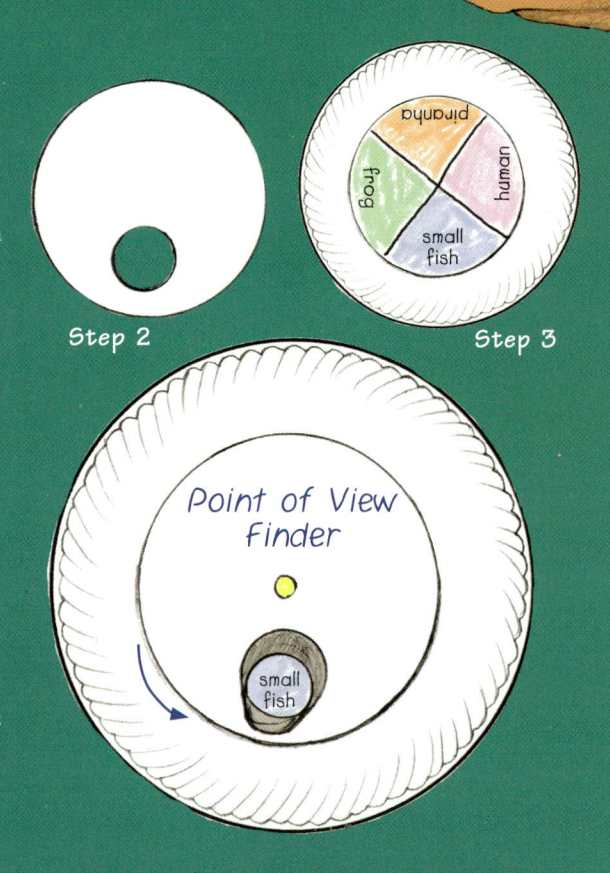

Step 2

Step 3

Point of View Finder

small fish

Eating Machines

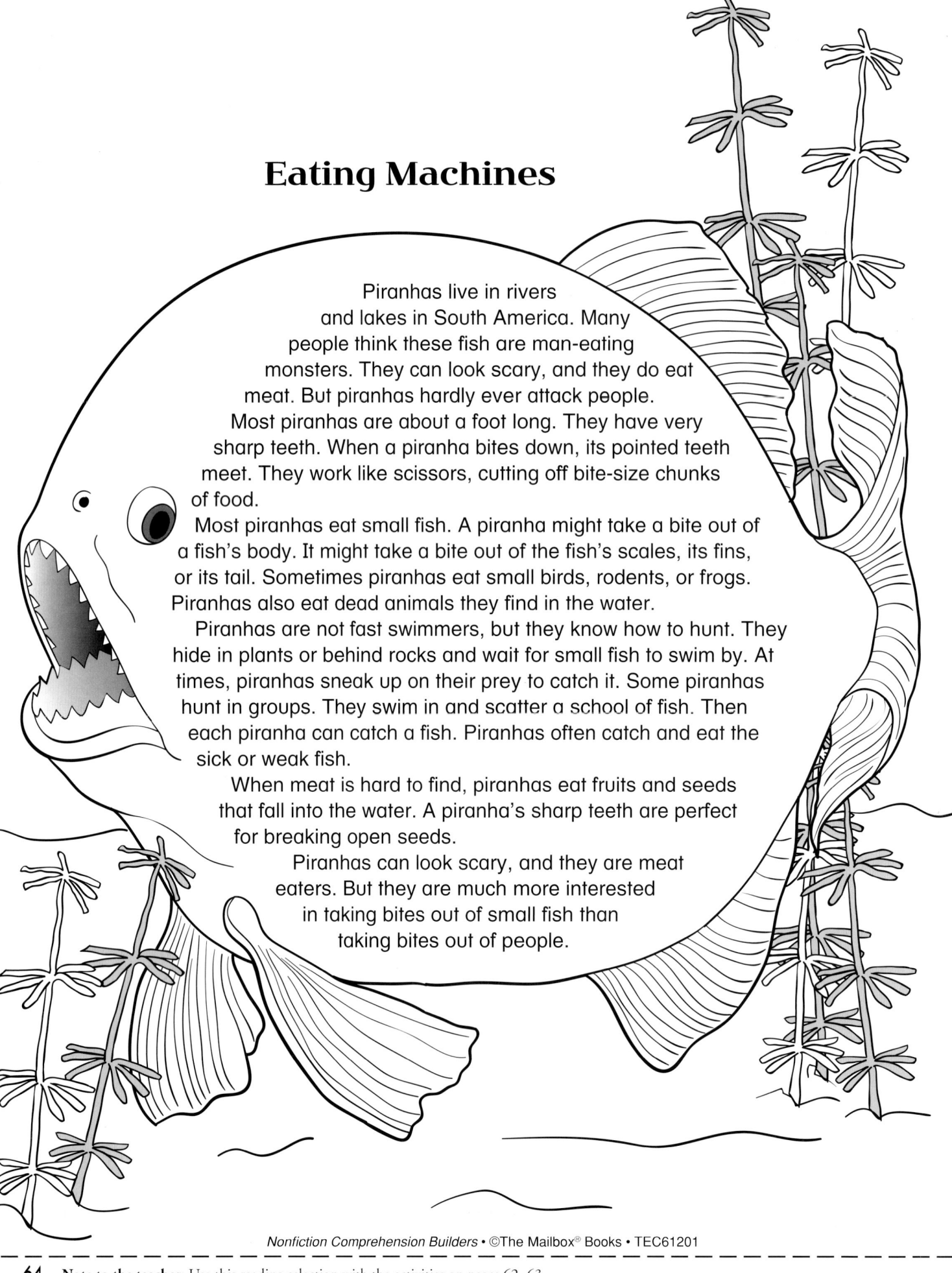

Piranhas live in rivers and lakes in South America. Many people think these fish are man-eating monsters. They can look scary, and they do eat meat. But piranhas hardly ever attack people.

Most piranhas are about a foot long. They have very sharp teeth. When a piranha bites down, its pointed teeth meet. They work like scissors, cutting off bite-size chunks of food.

Most piranhas eat small fish. A piranha might take a bite out of a fish's body. It might take a bite out of the fish's scales, its fins, or its tail. Sometimes piranhas eat small birds, rodents, or frogs. Piranhas also eat dead animals they find in the water.

Piranhas are not fast swimmers, but they know how to hunt. They hide in plants or behind rocks and wait for small fish to swim by. At times, piranhas sneak up on their prey to catch it. Some piranhas hunt in groups. They swim in and scatter a school of fish. Then each piranha can catch a fish. Piranhas often catch and eat the sick or weak fish.

When meat is hard to find, piranhas eat fruits and seeds that fall into the water. A piranha's sharp teeth are perfect for breaking open seeds.

Piranhas can look scary, and they are meat eaters. But they are much more interested in taking bites out of small fish than taking bites out of people.

Vocabulary Cards

Use with "Vocabulary" on page 62.

a part of a fish's body that sticks out and is used to swim and to steer	a freshwater fish with very sharp teeth
an animal that another animal hunts for food	thin, hard pieces that cover fish
to spread something out	a large group of the same kind of fish that swim together
fin	**piranha**
prey	**scales**
scatter	**school of fish**

"What About the Whydah?"

*with ideas by Kim T. Griswell, Honesdale, PA
and Rusty Fischer, Orlando, FL*

Making Predictions

Add another dimension to predicting with this simple idea. Read aloud the passage's first paragraph and then have each student write a one-sentence prediction about the fate of the *Whydah*. Collect the predictions, seal them in a plastic zipper bag, tape the bag to the board, and draw a pirate's treasure chest around the bag. Next, read aloud the rest of the passage. Then remove the bag from its chalkboard chest. Pull out each prediction, read it aloud, and guide students to compare it with the passage.

I think the pirates will sink the Whydah with their cannons.

Monitoring Comprehension

Try this tip to encourage students to stop and think about what they are reading. Guide each student to read the passage as if he were going to read it to a much younger student. As he reads, have him draw a speech bubble at each point in the passage where he might have to stop and explain something to a younger child. Then guide the student to write in the speech bubble what he would say before continuing to read. If possible, follow up by having each student read the passage with its side notes to a younger student. Everybody learns!

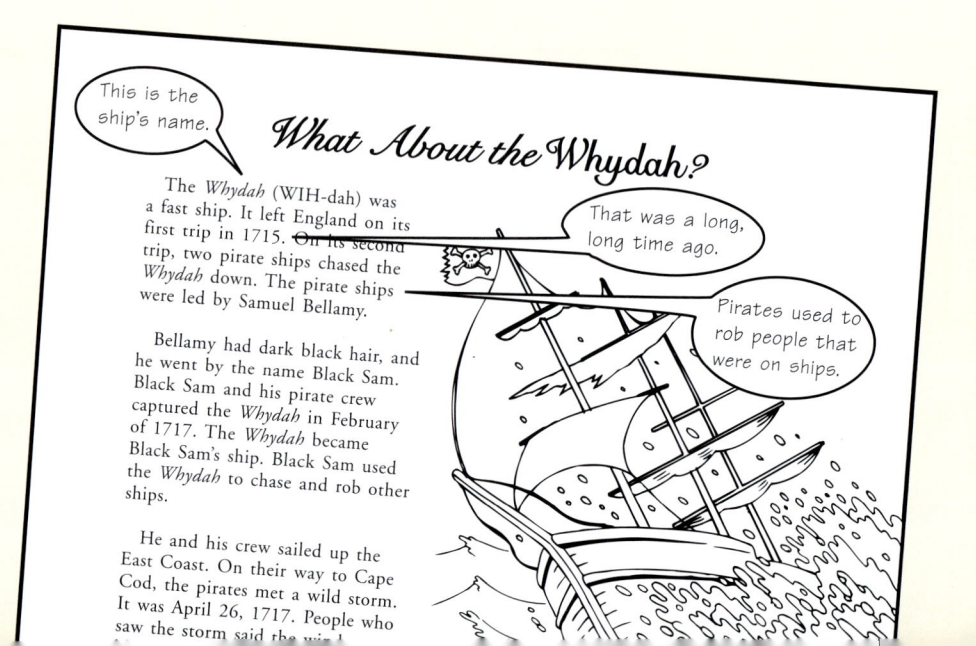

What About the Whydah?

This is the ship's name.

The *Whydah* (WIH-dah) was a fast ship. It left England on its first trip in 1715. On its second trip, two pirate ships chased the *Whydah* down. The pirate ships were led by Samuel Bellamy.

That was a long, long time ago.

Pirates used to rob people that were on ships.

Bellamy had dark black hair, and he went by the name Black Sam. Black Sam and his pirate crew captured the *Whydah* in February of 1717. The *Whydah* became Black Sam's ship. Black Sam used the *Whydah* to chase and rob other ships.

He and his crew sailed up the East Coast. On their way to Cape Cod, the pirates met a wild storm. It was April 26, 1717. People who saw the storm said the wi

Syllabication

Make syllable study a rich activity! Challenge each pair of students to find all of the two-syllable words in the passage. Provide construction paper scraps and have the duo write each word it finds on a coin-shaped cutout, listing each word only once. At the end of the session, have the partners count their coins to see who the richest word hunters are! *(There are 29 different two-syllable words in the passage.)*

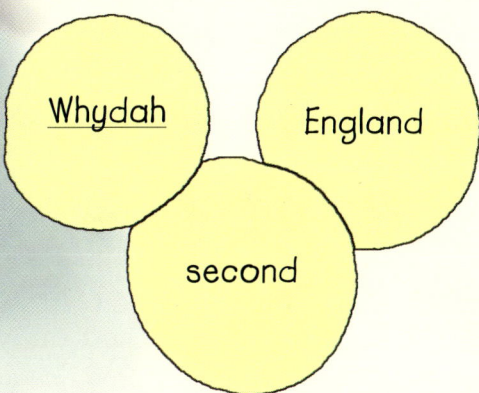

Whydah

England

second

Inferring

Help students learn to read between the lines! To begin, cut apart each paragraph from a copy of page 68 (enlarge if desired). Divide students into six groups and give each group one paragraph strip. Have the group glue its strip onto a sheet of unlined paper and illustrate the paragraph on the page. Post the finished pages in order on the board, placing a blank sheet of paper between each one and after the last one. Next, give each group one of the sheets of blank paper and have the students show on the page what they think happened between the two paragraphs or after the last paragraph. Then have students caption their drawings. To make an accordion-folded class book, tape together the finished pages and add construction paper covers as shown.

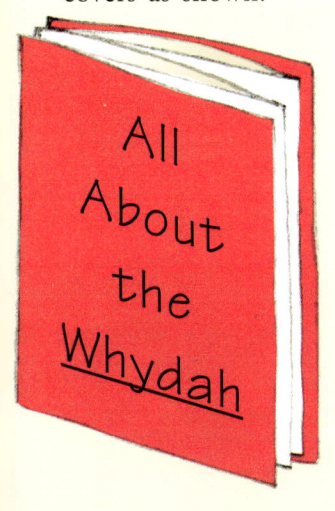

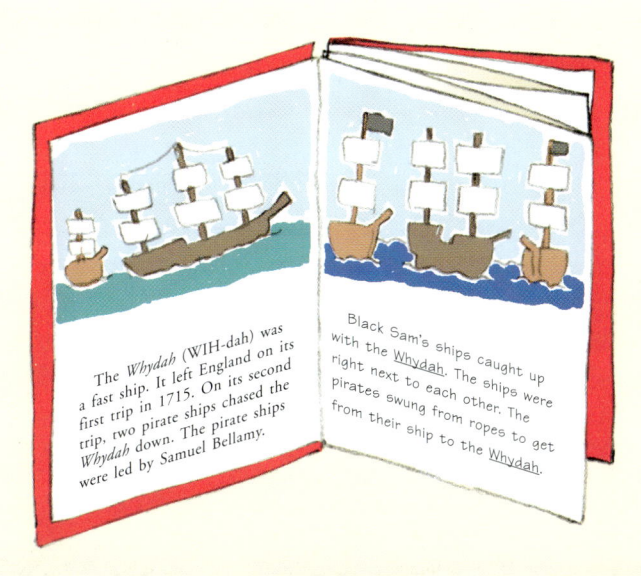

All About the Whydah

The *Whydah* (WIH-dah) was a fast ship. It left England on its first trip in 1715. On its second trip, two pirate ships chased the *Whydah* down. The pirate ships were led by Samuel Bellamy.

Black Sam's ships caught up with the *Whydah*. The ships were right next to each other. The pirates swung from ropes to get from their ship to the *Whydah*.

67

What About the Whydah?

The *Whydah* (WIH-dah) was a fast ship. It left England on its first trip in 1715. On its second trip, two pirate ships chased the *Whydah* down. The pirate ships were led by Samuel Bellamy.

Bellamy had dark black hair, and he went by the name Black Sam. Black Sam and his pirate crew captured the *Whydah* in February of 1717. The *Whydah* became Black Sam's ship. Black Sam used the *Whydah* to chase and rob other ships.

He and his crew sailed up the East Coast. On their way to Cape Cod, the pirates met a wild storm. It was April 26, 1717. People who saw the storm said the wind was blowing over 70 miles an hour. They said the waves were over 30 feet high. The *Whydah* was doomed.

A wild storm hits the *Whydah*.

The ship crashed into a sandbar. It broke apart and sank. Just about everything in the *Whydah* spilled into the ocean. Only two men lived through the shipwreck. One of them said there were 180 bags of gold and silver on the ship.

Many people tried to find riches from the ship. No one found the bags of gold and silver. Before long, the broken ship was lost in the sand.

More than 250 years later, divers found three cannons from the *Whydah*. It was July 20, 1984. Since then, a crew of treasure hunters has found over 100,000 items from the *Whydah*. They have found weapons the pirates used. They have found dishes and clothes. They have found coins. They have not found 180 bags of gold and silver, at least not yet.

A diver looks for the *Whydah*'s treasure.

Name _____

Sequencing

Setting Sail

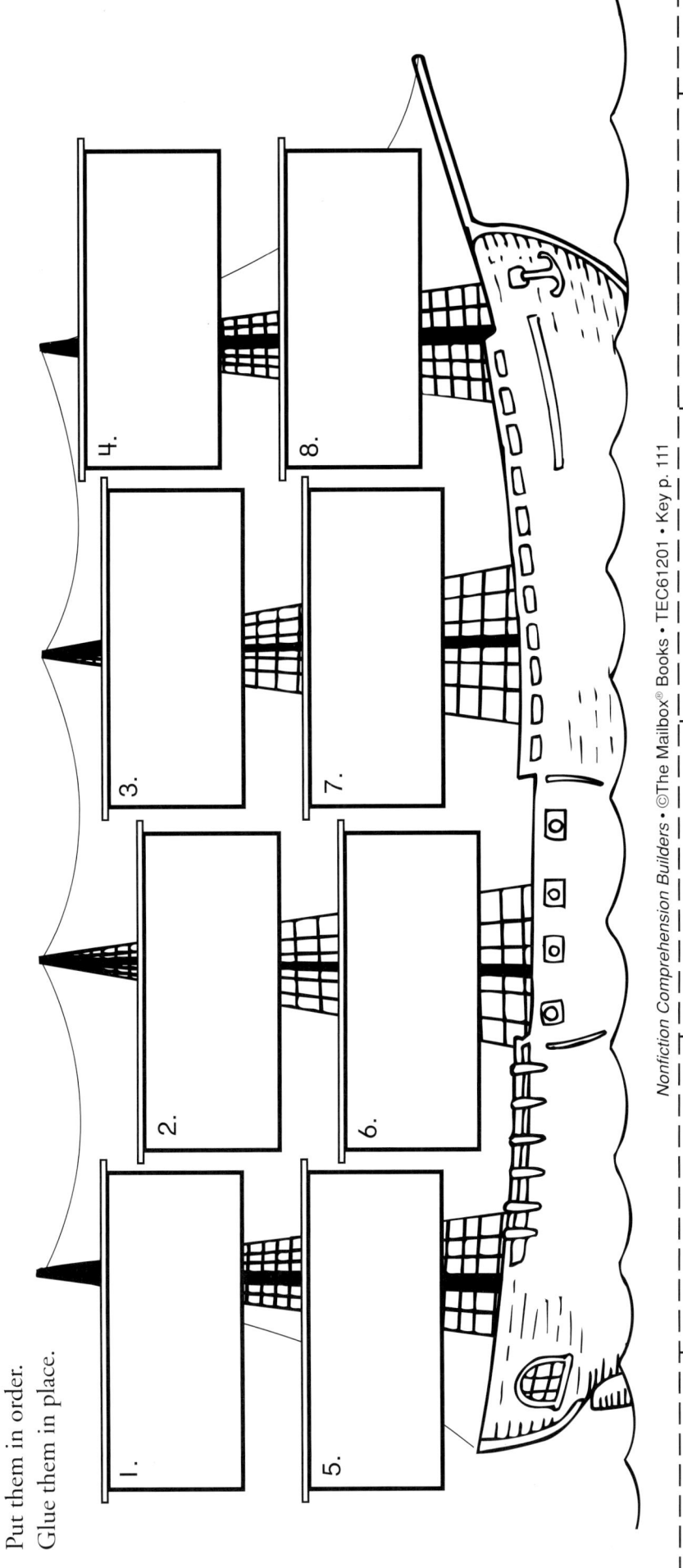

Cut out the boxes below.
Put them in order.
Glue them in place.

1.
2.
3.
4.
5.
6.
7.
8.

Nonfiction Comprehension Builders • ©The Mailbox® Books • TEC61201 • Key p. 111

| The *Whydah* leaves England on its first trip. | Sand buries the wrecked ship and its riches. | During the *Whydah*'s second trip, two pirate ships chase it. | The *Whydah* hits a bad storm, and it sinks. |
| Pirates use the *Whydah* to rob other ships. | Divers find three cannons that were on the *Whydah*. | Treasure hunters find over 100,000 items from the *Whydah*. | Black Sam and his crew capture the *Whydah*. |

Note to the teacher: Use with "What About the *Whydah*?" on page 68.

69

"In Search of the Strange"

reading selection by Kim T. Griswell, Honesdale, PA

Vocabulary

Make vocabulary exploration meaningful with this activity. First, copy the words listed onto a piece of chart paper. Direct each small group to define one word and create a quick skit to act out the word's meaning. Guide the class to guess which vocabulary word the group acts out and then create a definition that matches the group's actions. Record each definition on the paper, including stick figure sketches when possible. Leave the chart posted as students read the passage and complete the following activities.

strange: weird
scientists: people who study science
covered: spread over something else
explained: made something easy to understand
creature: an animal
giant: very, very big
extinct: no longer living
sloth: a really slow, hairy animal that lives in trees in South America

"Slow Sloth's Slow Song"
I......am......a......sloth......
a......sloth......am......I....

Building Background Knowledge

Get students into the comprehension act with this quick idea. Read aloud the poem "Slow Sloth's Slow Song" from Jack Prelutsky's *Something Big Has Been Here* (Greenwillow Books, 1990; 160 pp.; ISBN 0-688-06434-5). Reread the poem, guiding students to act it out as though they were sloths themselves. The poem's pacing and vivid imagery will help students understand that the giant ground sloth was very different from today's slow-moving sloths. If desired, after reading the passage, guide students to write poems in Prelutsky's style to describe the giant ground sloth.

Visualizing

Reread with students the paragraph that describes giant ground sloths and ask each child to study the picture on the page. Lead students to circle details from the paragraph that are evident in the illustration. Next, reread the Amazon hunters' quotations and the creature's description and have students circle the informative details. Then have each student fold up the bottom inch of a sheet of unlined paper. Guide him to draw a full-color illustration of the creature, unfold the paper, and caption his drawing in the folded space. Allow students to share their drawings before binding them together with a copy of the passage in a class book titled "In Search of the Strange."

The monster of the Amazon rain forest tears apart palm trees.

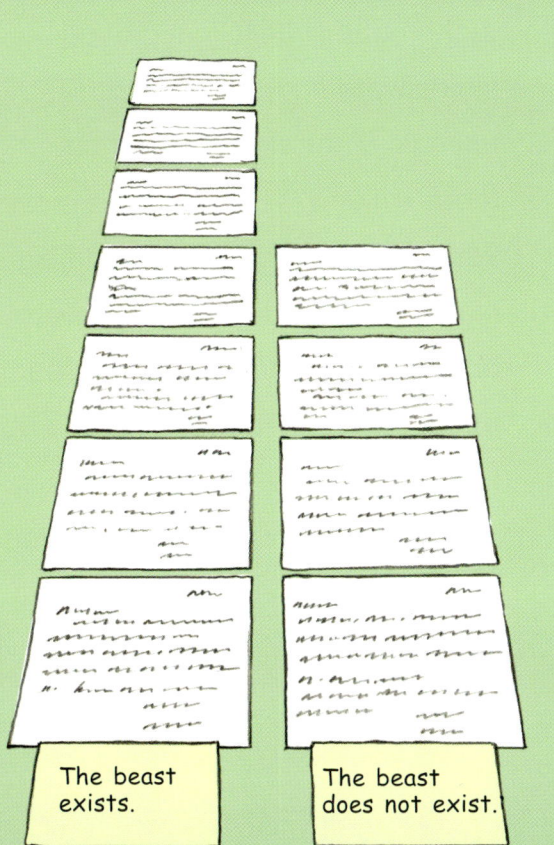

Synthesizing

After reading the selection, allow students to discuss the final questions with partners. Next, direct each student to decide whether or not she believes the mysterious Amazon creature exists. Announce that the scientist who believes that the beast is a giant ground sloth is named David Oren. Then guide each student to explain her point of view in a letter to Oren. Instruct the child to cite evidence from the passage to support her ideas. Allow students to share their letters, and place them in two columns to compare students' opinions.

The beast exists.

The beast does not exist.

In Search of the Strange

If you lived in the Amazon rain forest, you might hear stories about a strange, hairy beast. Scientists say the beast is only a legend. But people living in the forest say they have seen and heard the monster.

One Amazon hunter said, "I was working by the river when I heard a scream...." Then he saw what looked like a man coming out of the forest. He said it was covered in hair. It was walking on two legs like a man.

This model shows an extinct ground sloth.

"The moment you hear it, all your hairs stand on end," explained another hunter.

People along the Amazon have described the creature. They say it is covered in long red hair. When it stands up on its back legs, it is over six feet tall. Reports say the beast really stinks. It has huge claws that face backward. They say it is strong enough to tear apart a palm tree and eat its soft insides.

One scientist thinks the beast may be a giant ground sloth. Most scientists don't agree. Giant ground sloths became extinct around 10,000 years ago.

The Amazon beast seems a lot like a giant ground sloth. Giant ground sloths were huge, red-haired animals. They were faster than today's sloths. Today's sloths move very slowly. Ground sloths had big claws that curled under and faced backward. It seems that they stood up on their hind feet. They stood up to eat the leaves and twigs in trees.

What do you think? If you visited the Amazon rain forest, would you listen and look for a giant ground sloth?

Name _____   Comprehension

Strange Questions

Read "In Search of the Strange."
Shade the circle to show your answer.

1. Where is the Amazon rain forest?
   - (P) North America
   - (O) South America
   - (C) Pacific Ocean
   - (I) all of the above

2. According to the passage, the beast has
   - (T) long red hair and huge claws
   - (K) long white hair and huge claws
   - (L) short, messy hair
   - (U) no hair at all

3. According to the passage, who thinks the beast may be a giant ground sloth?
   - (N) one scientist
   - (D) no scientists
   - (Q) most scientists
   - (B) three scientists

4. Both the Amazon beast and the giant ground sloth
   - (E) stand up on their back legs
   - (W) have big claws
   - (H) have red hair
   - (M) all of the above

5. Why did the giant ground sloths stand up on their back legs?
   - (F) to tear apart trees
   - (R) to eat leaves and twigs in trees
   - (V) to stretch
   - (J) to get fruit

6. What is the last sentence in the reading passage?
   - (Y) a statement
   - (G) an exclamation
   - (I) a fragment
   - (S) a question

What could you call a very famous monster?
To find out, write each shaded letter on the matching line.

A "___ ___ ___ - ___ ___ A ___"!
     4 1 3   6 2   5

Nonfiction Comprehension Builders • ©The Mailbox® Books • TEC61201 • Key p. 111

Note to the teacher: Use with "In Search of the Strange" on page 72.

"Phantom Ships"

with ideas by Kim T. Griswell, Honesdale, PA, and Rusty Fischer, Orlando, FL

Building Background Knowledge

Before reading the selection on page 76, guide each student to follow the directions on page 77 to label the ship diagram. Next, have the child fold his paper in half, open it, and flip it to the blank side. Then read aloud the first paragraph of the selection on page 76. On the left half of his page, have each student draw a ghost ship as he pictures it. After reading the passage, have the student draw on the right half of the page a ghost ship that reflects the facts from the selection.

Writing a Legend

After reading, remind students that most legends start out as stories told and retold long before they are written down. Then guide each student to create a legend about a ship named after her that becomes a ghost ship. Next, have each pair of students tell each other the stories of their ghost ships. Then assign new partners and have each child tell her story to her new partner. Repeat one more time before having the student write her legend. After the child completes her draft, have her read it to a new partner and then revise it for the final retelling. To follow up, dim the lights and have each child read aloud her ghost ship legend.

Answering Open-Ended Questions

Make a transparency and a class supply of the selection on page 76. Also list on the board open-ended questions such as those shown. Next, read aloud each question, guiding students to discuss its answer and underline the text that supports it. Help students keep track of the underlined text by writing the matching question's number in the margin. Then have each child answer the questions on lined paper, being sure to cite text evidence.

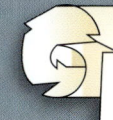

1. Were ghost ships haunted? Explain.
   (No, ghost ships were ships that had been abandoned. They were drifting on the open sea.)

2. Why did sailors abandon their ships? List three reasons.
   (Sailors abandoned their ships when they grew angry with the captain, when there was sickness on the ship, or when the ship was damaged.)

3. Why were ghost ships scary?
   (Ghost ships were scary because no one was steering them. Many ships crashed into ghost ships.)

4. Why do you think sailors told stories about ghost ships?
   (Answers will vary.)

Name _____ Supporting details

At Sea

List details from "Phantom Ships" to support this statement.

Ghost ships were scary, but they weren't haunted.

1. _____
2. _____
3. _____

Nonfiction Comprehension Builders • ©The Mailbox® Books • TEC61201

Note to the teacher: Use after reading "Phantom Ships" on page 76.

75

Phantom Ships

Sailors used to tell stories of scary ghost ships. They warned that phantom ships sailed the open seas. They believed the ships were manned by ghosts.

There really were ghost ships in the 1800s. But they weren't eerie ships haunted by ghosts. They were ships that were just drifting on ocean currents. They were ships that had been abandoned by their crews.

Ships were abandoned for many reasons. A group of sailors might grow angry at the captain. They might abandon or leave the ship. Some ships were abandoned when sickness spread among the sailors.

When they were damaged, the wooden ships of the 1800s were often abandoned. Ships were smashed in storms. They were burned in fires. They sprung leaks. Their masts broke. Even though the sailors abandoned their ships, some of the ships kept floating. They became ghost ships. Ghost ships drifted without crews to guide them. Some ghost ships floated on the open sea for years. Some ghost ships drifted for thousands of miles.

Coming up on a ghost ship wasn't just scary—it was dangerous. These ships weren't really haunted by ghosts. But with no one steering them, wrecks were likely. In the late 1800s, 21 ships crashed into ghost ships, and six of them sank. It's no wonder sailors told stories about scary ghost ships.

Name _____

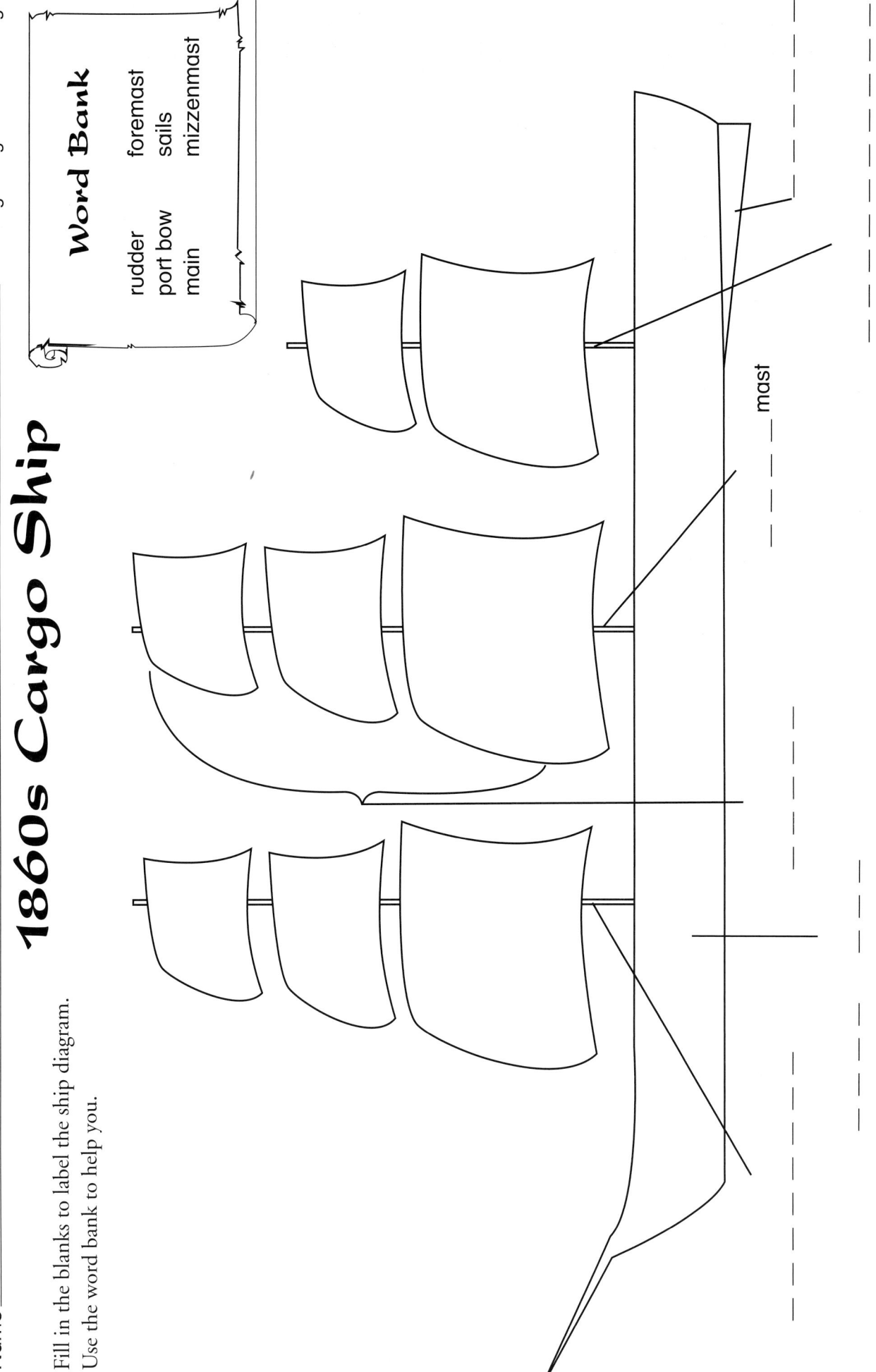

Building background knowledge

1860s Cargo Ship

Fill in the blanks to label the ship diagram. Use the word bank to help you.

Word Bank

rudder foremast sails
port bow mizzenmast
main

_____ mast

Note to the teacher: Use with "Building Background Knowledge" on page 74.

Nonfiction Comprehension Builders • ©The Mailbox® Books • TEC61201 • Key p. 111

77

"1600 'Pet-sylvania' Avenue"

reading selection by Kim T. Griswell, Honesdale, PA

Vocabulary

An independent or paired reading of the passage on page 80 works best for this vocabulary-boosting activity. Before students read the passage, prepare them for encountering unfamiliar words by posting and explaining the tips shown. Then direct students to take note of each unfamiliar word while reading and challenge them to use one or more of the tips displayed to better understand the word. As each student encounters an unknown word, he records the word, its meaning, and the number of the tip that was most helpful in understanding it. Allow readers to share their words, meanings, and most valuable tips used.

Tips to Try
1. Sound the word out.
2. Think about words that are similar.
3. Look for roots, parts, or base words.
4. Use a dictionary or a thesaurus.
5. Use context clues.

Fact and Opinion

Have your class create these stately graphic organizers for distinguishing fact and opinion. After students read the passage on page 80, remind them that facts can be proven or observed and that opinions are related to beliefs or feelings that cannot be proven. Then guide each student to draw an outline of the White House on a sheet of unlined paper, label one half of the outline "Facts," and then label the other half "Opinions" (as shown). Next, have readers revisit the passage one paragraph at a time. Have them list on the appropriate side of the outline one fact and one opinion inspired by each paragraph. If desired, have each student finish up her graphic organizer by adorning it with White House details, drawings of presidential pets, and a creative title.

Presidential Pets

| Facts | Opinions |

Drawing Conclusions

Readers will flip for this drawing-conclusions activity! After each student has read the passage, invite him to create a two-sided voting stick. To make a stick, direct each student to fold a large unruled index card in half. Keeping the fold at the top, have him write "valid" on the card in large letters. Have him flip the folded card and write "invalid" in the same manner. Then direct each child to tape a craft stick between the two halves before taping the halves closed.

Next, tell your class that good readers draw conclusions and support their conclusions with evidence from the text and personal experiences. Then share each conclusion shown one at a time. Each student flips his voting stick to demonstrate whether he feels the conclusion is valid or invalid based on his reading of the story. After it is determined how most of the class feels, invite students to share specific evidence from the text and personal experiences that prove the conclusion.

There's plenty of room for pets at the White House.
Lincoln and his son had a good relationship.
Calvin Coolidge and his wife were animal lovers.
Alice Roosevelt was a shy, quiet girl.
President Truman did not trust many people.

Summarizing

Ready. Set. Action! Put the final touches on students' study of this passage by having them summarize it in the form of a news broadcast. Divide students into pairs. Guide the students in each pair to identify the important details in the passage and put them into their own words (in order) to create a summary of the selection. Next, set up a mock news desk in front of a sign labeled "Presidential Pets: The Inside Scoop." Allow time for each pair to present its summary on the imaginary show *Inside the White House.* If desired, have students research other presidential pets not mentioned in the passage and present information about these pets as exclusives.

1600 "Pet-sylvania" Avenue

How do you turn the White House into an animal house? Open its doors to pets! The **mansion** known as the White House is big enough to house many first pets. It has 132 rooms! Barks, meows, and even hisses have come from some of those rooms.

Visitors to the East Room were in for a surprise when John Quincy Adams was president. Adams let a friend's alligator **lounge** in the East Room for two months in the summer of 1826.

President Lincoln's guests might have seen turkeys **strutting** around. One was supposed to be dinner at the White House. But Lincoln's son begged to keep the bird as a pet. After that, Jack the turkey gobbled around the White House grounds.

Another White House pet barely escaped becoming the main course. A raccoon was sent to President Coolidge for Thanksgiving dinner. However, when the president saw the animal's eyes, he had other plans for it! Coolidge named his new pet Rebecca and built a pen for her outside the Oval Office.

President Theodore Roosevelt's daughter Alice once brought Emily Spinach, her pet snake, to a party. Alice put the snake inside her purse. When the party got quiet, Alice opened her purse and let the snake out. Some of the guests ran from the room!

Emily Spinach wasn't the only first pet to make someone run. President Harrison gave his grandchildren a goat named His Whiskers. The goat pulled the children around the White House lawn in a little cart. One day, His Whiskers decided to see the world. He **bolted** out of the White House gate with the children. The president had to race after the cart.

What other pets have called 1600 Pennsylvania Avenue home? A lizard named Bill, a pig named Maude, and a dog named Grits are just a few of the 400 or so pets that have lived at America's most famous address. Nearly all the presidents have had pets. After all, as President Truman said, "If you want a friend in Washington, get a dog."

"A Magical Pen"

ideas by Terry Healy, Manhattan, KS
reading selection by Kim T. Griswell, Honesdale, PA

Making Predictions

Turn your students into star predictors! In advance, make five star-shaped cutouts and program each one with a different event from the story like the ones shown. Choose events that allow students to make predictions about the passage, such as what may happen next or what may happen as a result of the event. Before sharing the passage, tape one star on the board. Have a student volunteer read the information on the star; then encourage students to make predictions and discuss them. Record students' predictions on chart paper that has been taped below the appropriate star. Then repeat the activity with each remaining star.

After sharing the passage, revisit the predictions. Guide the class to confirm or revise each prediction according to the information they have read in the passage.

She kept library books past their due dates.

The memory of her teacher stayed in her brain.

Joanne liked to play witches and wizards with the Potter children.

Author's Purpose

Here's a hands-on way for readers to explore an author's purpose. Explain that authors have different purposes for writing passages. Authors may write to entertain, inform, or persuade. Guide students in a discussion of each of these purposes. For example, an author may write an entertaining passage to make the reader laugh. An author may write an informative passage to tell the reader information about a specific topic. Or an author may write a persuasive passage to influence the reader's opinion about a specific topic. Next, give each child a copy of page 84 and the passage on page 83. Help her number the paragraphs in the passage from 1 to 6. Have her refer to the numbered paragraphs as she follows the directions on page 84 to complete the page. Once students have completed the page, lead them in a discussion of their work. If desired, collect the pages and redistribute them so that students can complete the summarizing activity on page 82.

Vocabulary

When she was six, J. K. Rowling wrote a book about a rabbit. Help your students increase their vocabulary skills when they make these rabbit-shaped books! Enlarge the rabbit pattern on this page so that it is eight inches wide. Trace the enlarged pattern on tagboard and then cut it out to make a rabbit-shaped template. Next, each child uses the template to make six rabbit cutouts out of construction paper. On each cutout, she writes a different boldfaced word from the passage. Then she writes a short definition of the word, using a dictionary as necessary. Finally, she writes an original sentence that includes the word. She staples the completed pages together to create an at-a-glance vocabulary reference!

fines—money paid for breaking rules

Sandy owed $2.25 in fines for turning in her library books late.

TEC61201

Summarizing

Students are sure to want to use these summaries-in-the-round to tell the story of J. K. Rowling's life again and again! To begin, give each child his completed copy of page 84. Have him review the facts and then write a short summary of J. K. Rowling's life. In addition, encourage him to refer to the passage as necessary. Next, give the child an empty paper towel tube and a 1" x 18" white paper strip. Help him copy his summary onto the strip. Then have him tape the strip around the tube as shown. To add colorful details to his project, direct the child to draw small symbols of Joanne's life on white paper. Have him cut out the symbols, color them, and glue each one onto his tube. Invite the child to take his circular summary home and use it to share the story of J. K. Rowling with his family.

A Magical Pen

Joanne was a quiet, freckly, shortsighted kid who was not good at sports. Most of the time, she had her nose stuck in a book. She kept library books long past their due dates. In fact, she ran up some large **fines**. When she wasn't reading, she was writing or telling stories to her sister, Dianne. At the age of six, Joanne wrote her first book. It was called *Rabbit*. The rabbit had the measles. He had a friend named Miss Bee. "It's weird," Joanne says, "but writing is all I ever wanted to do."

When she was nine, Joanne went to an **old-fashioned** school. Her teacher gave Joanne a math test on her first day in class. Joanne missed ten out of ten questions. The teacher moved her to the right side of the room. Joanne realized that all of the students on that side were not doing well in school. It took a lot of hard work for Joanne to move to the other side of the room.

The memory of her teacher stayed in Joanne's brain, as did the memory of her childhood friends Ian and Vikki Potter. Joanne liked to play witches and wizards with the Potter children. Another memory she tucked away was of her best friend, Sean, and his **turquoise** car. As she got older, Joanne's memories burst out into her writing.

Quiet, freckled Joanne is J. K. Rowling. She is the author of the Harry Potter books. The idea for Harry came to Joanne one day as she was stuck on a train. She was staring out the window at some cows. Then Harry and the wizard school popped into her mind. By the end of the trip she had the basic idea for the first Harry Potter book.

Joanne won't tell, but her old-fashioned teacher may have been in her mind as she wrote about Professor Snape, the **strict** teacher at Harry's school. Harry's last name came from the **surname** of the Potter children. His friend Ron comes from Joanne's memories of Sean. Ron and Harry's ride in a magical car is based on Sean's car.

"Write about your own **experiences** and your own feelings," Joanne tells young writers. That's what she does. She uses her pen like a magic wand. She turns her memories into stories that are loved by readers all over the world.

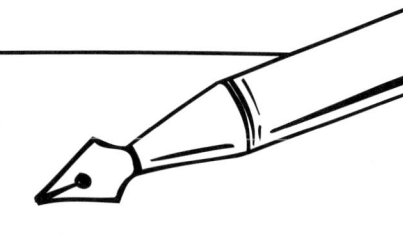

Name _____ Discovering an author's purpose

Why Write?

For each numbered paragraph, write one fact about Joanne K. Rowling.

Paragraph 1: _____
_____

Paragraph 2: _____
_____

Paragraph 3: _____
_____

Paragraph 4: _____
_____

Paragraph 5: _____
_____

Paragraph 6: _____
_____

Do you think "A Magical Pen" was written to entertain, inform, or persuade?
_____

Why? _____
_____
_____

Nonfiction Comprehension Builders • ©The Mailbox® Books • TEC61201

84 **Note to the teacher:** Use with "Author's Purpose" on page 81 and "Summarizing" on page 82.

"Bloodsucking Pests"

reading selection by Kim T. Griswell, Honesdale, PA

Lice
Lice can live on peoples' heads.

Activating Prior Knowledge
Sharing what they know about bloodsucking pests before they read engages students in the learning process! Make a transparency of page 87. Display the transparency so that only the title and art are visible. Lead students in a discussion of what they see, pointing out the mosquito, the tick, and the louse. Prompt students to think about what they already know about these creatures. Next, give each child a 4½" x 6" piece of construction paper. Have him trim the paper so that it looks like the creature of his choice. Have him write the creature's name and a sentence telling something he knows about it. After each child shares his sentence with the class, tape his creature onto a large jar-shaped cutout. Title the display "What We Know About Creepy-Crawly Creatures."

Reading for Details
Send students on a fact hunt to increase their understanding of the passage! Give each child a copy of page 88 and a copy of the passage on page 87. Instruct her to scan the passage to find phrases that describe each creature. Have her record her findings on her copy of page 88. Provide time for each child to compare her work with a partner's.

Fact and Opinion

This fact-filled passage is sure to inspire your students to share their opinions about bloodsucking pests! Have each pair of students draw a two-column chart with headings like the ones shown. Next, direct students to reread the passage, looking for facts. Have partners take turns recording each one in the appropriate column until a predetermined number have been found. Then direct each partner to record at least three of his own opinions in the appropriate column.

Just the Facts!	Just Our Opinions!
• There are at least 60 different types of leeches in the United States. • Leeches can live in lakes and streams.	• A leech bite would hurt! • Leeches are gross!

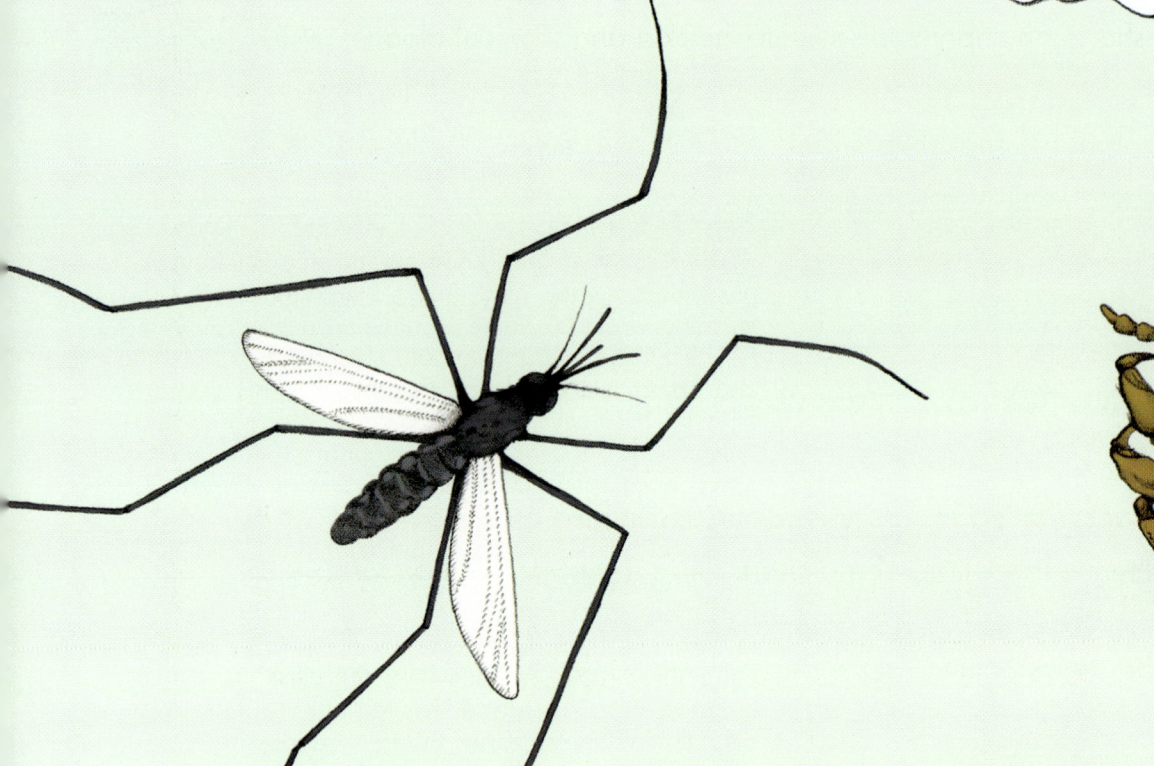

Questioning

Keep the questions coming with an exciting round of Pass the Pest! In advance, copy the mosquito pattern on this page to make four mosquito cutouts. Direct each student to write a question about bloodsucking pests. Explain to students that each question's answer must be contained within the passage. To play, have four student volunteers each hold a mosquito cutout and stand in front of the classroom. Next, have one seated student ask the first standing child a question. If the child doesn't know the answer, she passes her cutout to the questioner and returns to her seat. The questioner then takes her place at the front of the room. If the student answers the question correctly, she remains in place. Continue until all the students' questions have been answered, and remind students to ask questions about their reading even when there's no pest to pass!

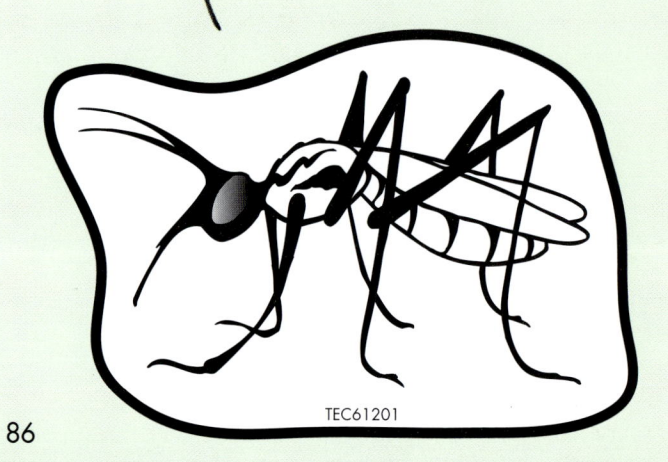

TEC61201

Bloodsucking Pests

Bloodsuckers are all around us. They are in the air, on the ground, in the water—everywhere! What are these pests? They are parasites. They feast on the blood of living creatures. Most of the time, they don't hurt the creature.

At least 60 different kinds of leeches live in lakes and streams in the United States. These slimy worms have flat, narrow bodies. Some are shorter than half an inch. Others are as long as 20 inches. A leech attaches itself to a warm body. Then it uses its sharp mouthparts to saw into the skin and suck out blood.

Despite their strange eating habits, leeches aren't all bad. They have been used to suck the poison out of snakebites. Their saliva may help prevent blood clots in humans and speed healing.

Another creature that feeds on blood is the louse. Lice are wingless insects. They can live on mammals and birds. Their tiny pale bodies make them hard to see. They use the curved claws at the ends of their legs to cling to hair, feathers, or fur. Lice use their long, hollow beaks to suck up blood.

Leeches and lice aren't the only bloodsucking pests. Ticks hang out in fields, deserts, and woods waiting for animals or humans to pass by. A tick sticks out its front legs and then catches hold of a passerby with its claws. The tick burrows its head under its host's skin. Then it sucks blood and swells up like a balloon.

Not all bloodsuckers crawl or swim. The mosquito flies. It has two wings, six long legs, and a small body. The female has a long, hollow mouth that contains a sucking tube. The female mosquito finds a soft spot on a host's skin and begins feeding. She is done in about two minutes, but her bite has a chemical that keeps the host itching for much longer.

The next time you feel that itchy, creepy feeling, take a close look! You may have a bloodsucking pest along for the ride.

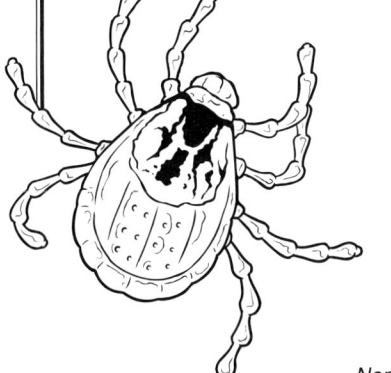

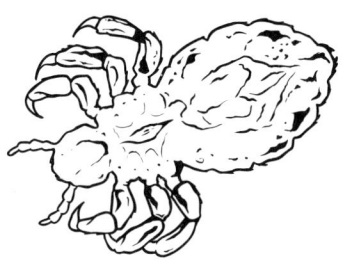

Name _____   Reading for details

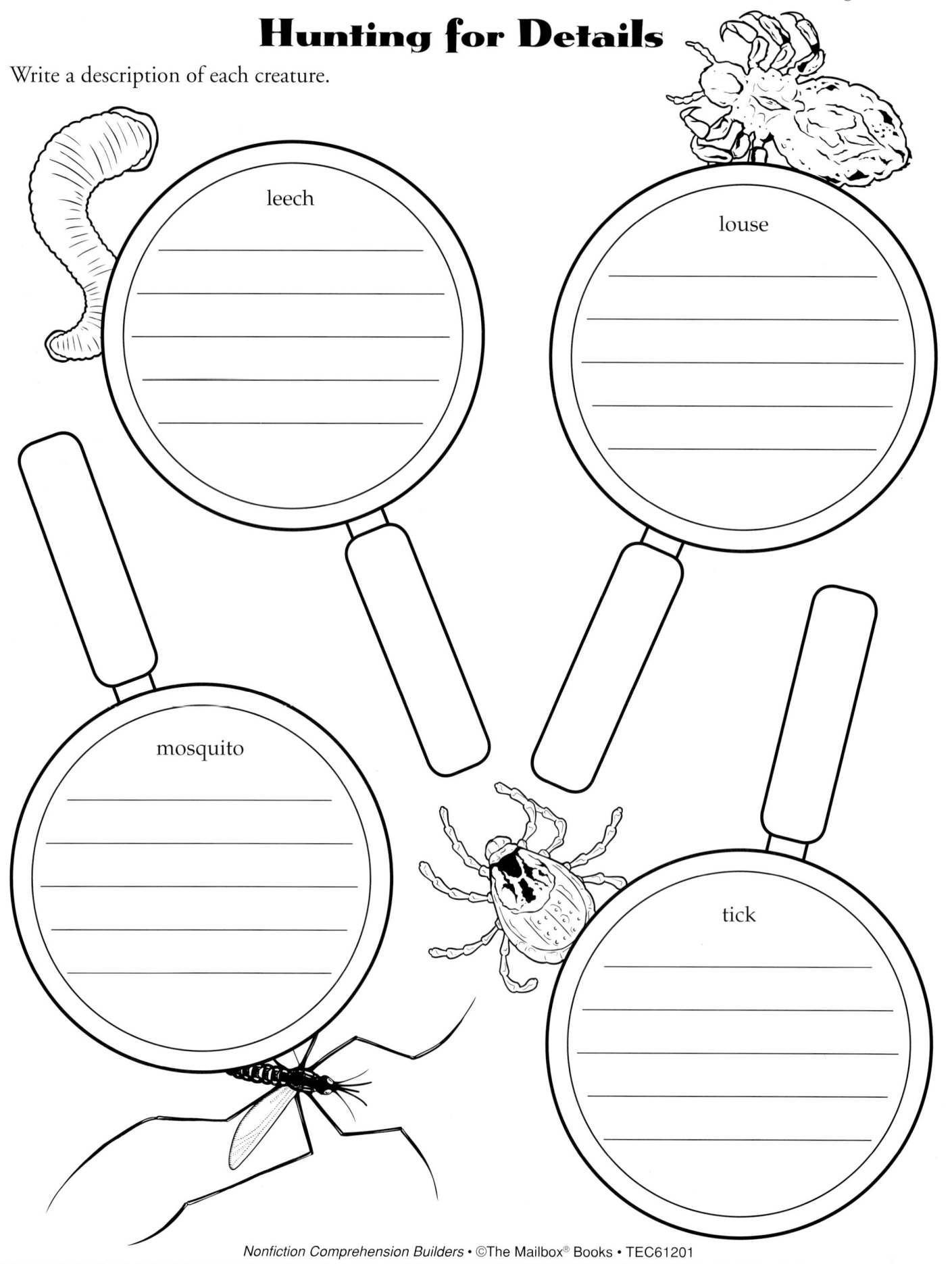

Hunting for Details

Write a description of each creature.

leech
_____
_____
_____
_____

louse
_____
_____
_____
_____

mosquito
_____
_____
_____
_____

tick
_____
_____
_____
_____

"Hiding in Plain View"

*reading selection by Kim T. Griswell, Honesdale, PA
with ideas by Colleen Dabney, Williamsburg, VA*

Vocabulary

Can you picture students reading science-related terms with ease? They will when you use this prereading activity! Have students create a picture dictionary using the italicized words from the passage on page 91. Pair students and assign one word to each pair. Provide each twosome with access to a print or online dictionary, thesaurus, and encyclopedia to research its term. Remind students to seek the science-related meaning for each word. When research is complete, instruct each pair to write its word atop an unlined sheet of paper and include a matching illustration and definition underneath. Have students share their findings before posting the papers in ABC order. Now when it's time to read, students will feel confident about encountering scientific words.

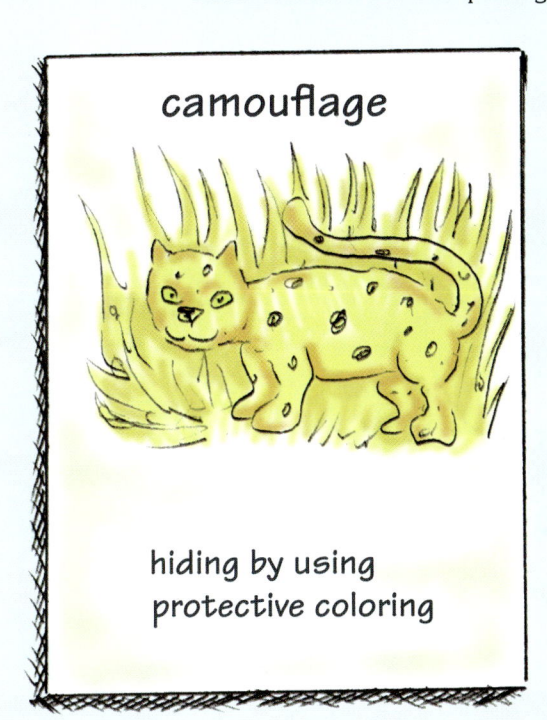

camouflage

hiding by using protective coloring

Categorizing

Here's an easy way to help readers classify and organize information. After an initial reading of the passage on page 91, explain to students that good readers look for and organize related details. Identifying similar ideas helps the reader better understand and remember information. Next, give each student a copy of page 92. Guide students in completing Step 1 of the activity. Then, before each student completes Step 2, instruct him to reread the passage, this time paying close attention to facts that relate to the category headings. Upon completion of the activity, have each student join a classmate to share and compare her findings.

Comparing and Contrasting

After students have completed the reproducible activity on page 92, invite them to "tri" making three-way comparisons. Draw three overlapping circles to create a Venn diagram on the chalkboard. Familiarize students with how to use the diagram, and then divide them into groups to draw a model of the diagram on chart paper. Next, instruct each group to select three animals mentioned in the passage and label each circle with an animal. Then have the students reread "Hiding in Plain View" and work together to fill in as many sections of the diagram as possible that show similarities and differences among the three creatures. Remind students that all details will not be stated directly in the text. Challenge them to also think about how the items compare and contrast based on inferences drawn from the reading.

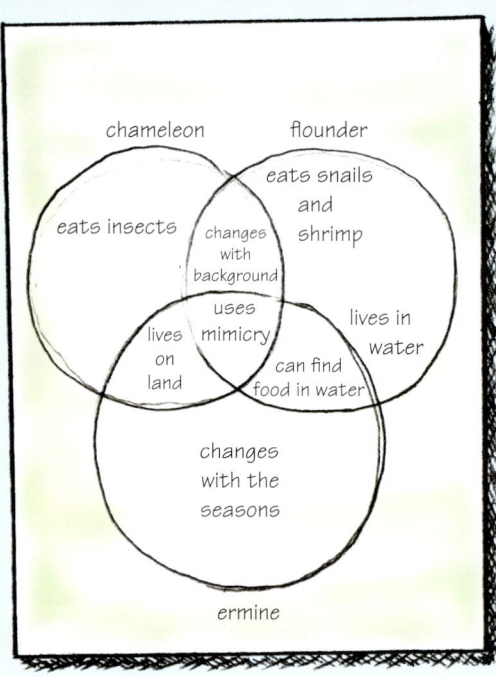

Venn diagram:
- chameleon: eats insects
- flounder: eats snails and shrimp
- ermine: changes with the seasons
- chameleon ∩ flounder: changes with background
- chameleon ∩ ermine: lives on land
- flounder ∩ ermine: can find food in water
- center: uses mimicry
- flounder: lives in water

Reading for Details

Having students aid in creating a quiz and answer key to accompany the reading selection is sure to get them reading for details! Divide the passage into five sections; then divide students into five groups. Assign each group a section of the passage. Instruct each group to randomly determine two true and two false statements related to the details in its section. Then instruct each group to write the statements on a sheet of chart paper, indicating the answers in order on the back of the chart. Mount the completed charts on the chalkboard and number the questions from 1 to 20. Then direct each student to independently practice reading for details by having him number his paper and use a copy of the passage to help him complete the quiz.

Hiding in Plain View

Hide and live—that is what some *animals* do. *Scientists* call hiding in plain view *mimicry*. Animals that practice mimicry hide by changing color or using shapes. Some change color quickly. Some change slowly. Some change with the seasons. Others have a shape to match their *environment*.

Nature's best change artist has to be the *chameleon*. This animal can be found in different forests. It uses its toes and tail to pull itself along as it waits for *insects*. Its green skin can change to brown or many different colors. Changing color makes it easy for the animal to sneak up on its *prey*.

There's something fishy about the *flounder*. Like the chameleon, it can change color. This fish may turn white and brown to match pebbles and shells at the bottom of the sea. It can turn gray to match harbor mud. It can even show spots or stripes. The flounder hides really well. If a *snail* or *shrimp* comes too close, it becomes a snack.

Unlike the chameleon and flounder, the *ermine* does not change quickly. It changes with the seasons. Most of the year this animal is mainly brown. It matches the fields, woods, and bushes where it lives. When winter comes, the ermine turns mostly white. It blends in with the snow. This helps the ermine get away from *predators* when it comes out to hunt for mice, fish, or eggs.

The *peppered moth* has changed color over time to match its environment. Most wear pale white or gray *camouflage*. Their wings have dark brown or black dots. Some are dark in color. The moth can blend in where it lives. It can match light colors in the forest or the dark colors of a polluted city.

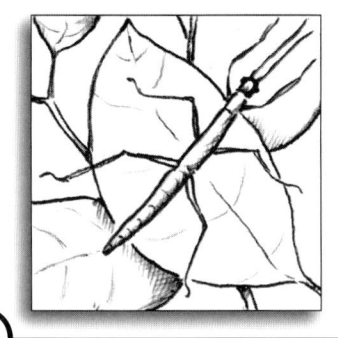

Changing color isn't the only way animals hide. Some use their shape. The *walking stick* lives in trees and bushes. This green or brown animal can look like a leaf or twig. Some walking sticks can also change color.

Whether they change color or use their shape, animals who use mimicry can be tough to spot. By hiding in plain view, these animals live to hide another day!

Nonfiction Comprehension Builders • ©The Mailbox® Books • TEC61201

Note to the teacher: Use this reading selection with the activities on pages 89, 90, and 92.

Name _____   Categorizing

Sort It Out!

Step 1: For each column, study the details from "Hiding in Plain View." Think about what they have in common. Write a category heading for the column. One has been done for you.

Step 2: Find information from the text that fits each category to complete the chart.

				How It Hides
chameleon	in the forest	insects		changes to brown or other colors quickly
flounder	in the sea	snails, shrimp		
ermine			mainly brown	
peppered moth		not given		has changed color over time to match its environment
walking stick			green or brown	

Bonus Box: If people asked you how to categorize information, what would you tell them? Write what you would say to make them understand.

Nonfiction Comprehension Builders • ©The Mailbox® Books • TEC61201 • Key p. 111

92   Note to the teacher: Use with "Categorizing" on page 89.

An Accidental Writer

reading selection by Kim T. Griswell, Honesdale, PA

Vocabulary

Before reading, introduce students to the story's vocabulary—and give practice using context clues too! Write each boldfaced word from the selection on page 95 on an index card. Then share each word with the class. Next, use the word in a sentence and challenge students to guess its meaning. (See sample sentences below.) If needed, use the word in more sentences until its meaning is determined. Finally, to help students remember what the word means, lead the class to determine a place in the classroom related to the meaning and mount the word card in that location. For example, students might decide that the word *incident* should be mounted near the TV because they learn about a variety of incidents (or events) while watching TV.

Sample Sentences
Mom has a *knack* for making babies smile.
I don't remember that *incident* happening.
The soldiers' *khaki* uniforms blend with the environment.
Thankfully, the man was *rescued* from the quicksand.
A descriptive *account* of the event is in the newspaper.

Reasons to Write

To Entertain
- asks interesting questions
- includes fun phrases

To Inform
- tells where the author lived
- tells how the author started writing

Author's Purpose

Help students determine the author's purpose in "An Accidental Writer" with this small-group activity. Remind students that authors write to inform, persuade, or entertain the reader. In this selection, the author combines two purposes—to inform and entertain. Next, direct each group to decorate and label a pencil-shaped cutout as shown. Then have students find evidence in the selection showing what the author wrote for each purpose. After each group has recorded its examples on its cutout, provide time for students to share supporting evidence.

93

Cause and Effect

Determining cause-and-effect relationships will be in the bag when you use this whole-group activity! In advance, write causes like those shown on strips of paper. Then place the strips inside a paper bag. After reading the selection, explain to students that the *cause* is why something happened and that the *effect* is what happened. Next, choose a student to draw one strip from the bag and read it to the class. Challenge other students in the class to generate possible effects of the cause based on the selection's content. Finally, if desired, challenge each student to think of an effect, write it on a strip of paper, and place it inside the bag. Then continue in the same manner as before with students suggesting causes for the effects.

- Forester took Dahl to lunch.
- Dahl joined the air force.
- Dahl's teachers did not like his writing.
- Dahl offered to write his story.
- Dahl had headaches.
- Dahl was in a plane crash.
- The weather in Africa was hot.
- Dahl's war story was great.

Making Judgments

Readers will be able to make valid judgments about Roald Dahl when you use this partner activity. Pair students and have each pair create a three-column chart with the following labels for the columns: "Believe," "Don't Believe," and "Not Sure." Write the statements below on the board. Ask each pair to determine whether they believe the statement, don't believe the statement, or are not sure whether to believe it. Then direct students to record the statement in the corresponding column of the chart. Ask each pair to explain its decision for each statement, citing at least one detail from the selection that supports the pair's judgment.

Dahl had a great imagination.
Dahl wanted to stop flying.
Dahl was a good pilot.
Dahl knew that Forester would like his story.
Dahl was from Great Britain.

An Accidental Writer

Do you know Matilda? She's a smart little girl with a **knack** for getting the better of mean Miss Trunchbull. How about the Big Friendly Giant? His heart is as big as his great big feet. What about James? He rolls away in a giant peach with a bunch of giant bugs!

If you know these characters, then you know something about Roald Dahl. You know that he was an author with a sharp sense of humor. But you may not know that he didn't plan to become an author. It was just a lucky break!

Such a successful writer must have dreamed of growing up and writing books, right? He must have written great papers in English class. Surely he always knew that he wanted to become an author. Not quite!

In school, Dahl's teachers said awful things about his writing. One even said that he always wrote the opposite of what he meant! So how could Dahl grow up to write books? According to him, it was all a lucky **incident** that happened after a not-so-lucky accident.

After leaving school, Dahl didn't want to write. He wanted to travel. He worked for an oil company in Africa. The weather was very hot. Instead of wearing a stuffy old suit, he could wear **khaki** shorts and an open shirt to work. He loved it!

While Dahl was in Africa, Britain went to war with Germany. Dahl joined Britain's air force and trained as a fighter pilot. During the war, his plane was shot down. Dahl was **rescued,** but badly hurt. Eventually, he had to stop flying because of headaches caused by his injuries. That led to Dahl's lucky break.

A famous writer, C. S. Forester, wanted to publish Dahl's war story in a magazine called the *Saturday Evening Post.* The two met for lunch so Dahl could share his experiences. Dahl tried to talk and eat. Forester tried to take notes and eat. It didn't work very well. So Dahl offered to write about his **account** and send it to Forester. Dahl couldn't believe the note Forester sent back about his story.

"I'm bowled over," it said. "Your piece is marvelous. It is the work of a gifted writer."

Could this be the same person whose teachers thought he was a terrible writer? Indeed it could! The *Saturday Evening Post* bought Dahl's story for $1,000, and the rest is writing history!

Dahl once said that all a writer needs is what he has in his head, a pencil, and a bit of paper. But it looks like a lucky break might help!

"Taking a Seat for Change"

ideas by Kathleen Scavone, Middletown, CA
reading selection by Kim T. Griswell, Honesdale, PA

Sequencing

Retelling the event in pictures gives students greater insight into the passage. To begin, lead students to discuss the sequence of events, beginning with Rosa taking a seat on the bus and ending with the Supreme Court's decision. Next, give each child a strip of adding machine tape. Direct him to draw a box and then illustrate the first event as shown. Have him continue in this manner until he has retold the entire passage. Display the completed strips on a bulletin board titled "Picturing Rosa Parks' Story."

Identifying Important Details

Teamwork makes this small-group reading activity great! Give each pair of students in a small group a copy of the passage on page 98 and a copy of the bus pattern on page 99. Next, assign each duo a section of the passage on page 98. Direct the twosome to skim its section to search for important details. As each detail is found, have the pair record it on its bus pattern. Once the partners are finished, read the passage aloud. As you read each duo's section, invite the partners to share their work.

Character's Point of View

Help students understand Rosa Parks' point of view with this three-dimensional writing project. Give each child a six-inch square of writing paper. Direct the child to imagine that she is Rosa Parks as she writes a paragraph explaining why Rosa stayed in her seat that day. Next, provide each student with the materials listed below and guide her through the directions to publish her writing. Then allow students to share their work with the class.

Materials for each student: 6" x 12" colored construction paper rectangle, 9" x 12" construction paper sheet, crayons, scissors, glue

Steps:
1. Place the rectangle on your desk horizontally. Fold the ends inward to meet in the middle.
2. Glue the writing inside the folds and refold the flaps.
3. Cut out a bus shape from the construction paper and decorate it.
4. Fold the cutout in half and cut the halves apart on the fold line.
5. Glue one half of the bus on each flap as shown.

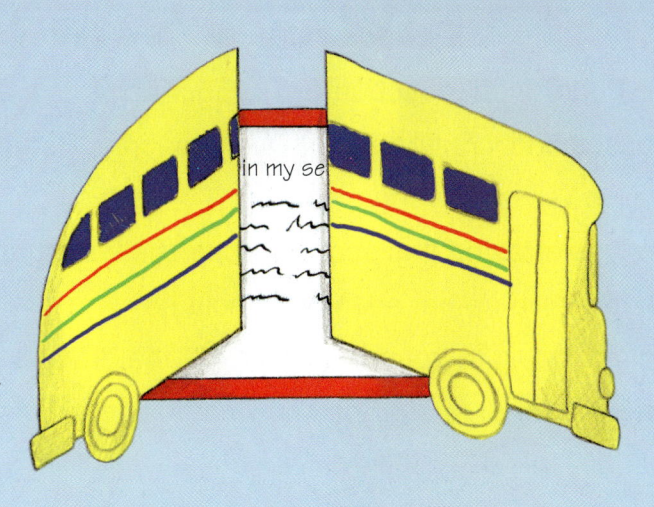

Synonyms

Looking for a synonym center that's simple and skill-based? This is your stop! To prepare, make ten copies of the bus and bus stop sign patterns on page 99. Cut out the patterns and program each bus with a word from the first column. Then program each bus stop sign with a word from the second column. Pair each bus with its matching sign and make them self-checking by putting like-colored dots on the backs of each pair's pieces. Mix up the pieces and place them at a center.

Instruct each student who visits the center to match the word on each bus with its synonym on a bus stop sign. Then have the child turn the pieces over to check his work.

kind	sweet
shout	yell
apart	separated
tired	weary
quiet	silent
grown-ups	adults
looking	watching
stared	gazed
frown	scowl
brave	courageous

Taking a Seat for Change

Rosa Parks lived in Alabama in 1955. The state's Jim Crow laws said that black people riding on buses had to sit apart from white people. People were looking for ways to prove that the Jim Crow laws were wrong.

Rosa was arrested that year because she would not stand on the bus. When the bus driver asked her to give up her seat, Rosa said no.

"Well, I'm going to have you arrested," the driver said.

Rosa knew what to do. She knew not to shout. She knew not to frown. She said, "You may do that."

Why would Rosa let herself be arrested because of a bus seat? She was on her way home from work. She was tired. But she did not stay in her seat because her feet were tired. She sat because she was tired of giving in.

Rosa's quiet act made other people brave enough to do something.

"Oh, she's so sweet. They've messed with the wrong one now!" said a girl watching Rosa at the courthouse. She stared at Rosa. How could a kind woman like her have to stand in front of a judge?

After Rosa's arrest, people handed out notices all over town. "We are…asking every Negro to stay off the buses Monday," the notices read. "Children and grown-ups, don't ride the bus at all on Monday."

More black people than white people rode the buses. If black people did not ride the buses, it would cost the bus companies a lot of money. Maybe the bus companies would change their rules. For more than a year, many black people did not ride public buses. Parents walked to work. Children walked to school.

After a year, the U.S. Supreme Court said that it was against the law to treat people in a different way on buses because of their skin color. Rosa Parks could not have agreed more!

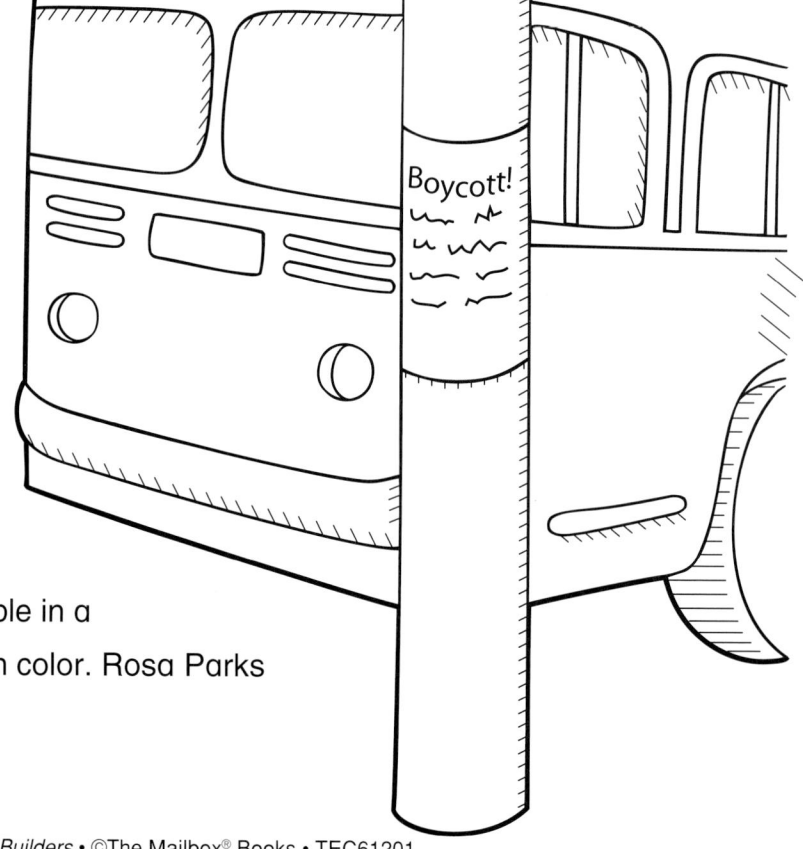

Bus Stop Sign Pattern
Use with "Synonyms" on page 97.

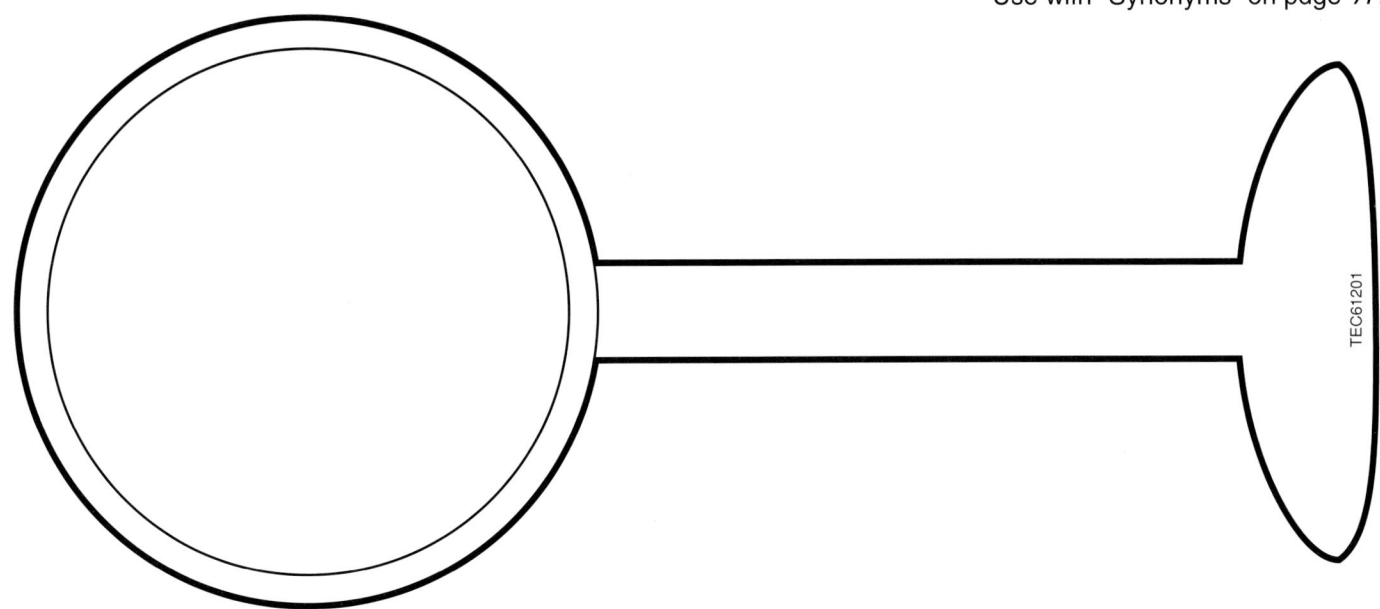

Bus Pattern
Use with "Identifying Important Details" on page 96 and "Synonyms" on page 97.

Nonfiction Comprehension Builders • ©The Mailbox® Books • TEC61201

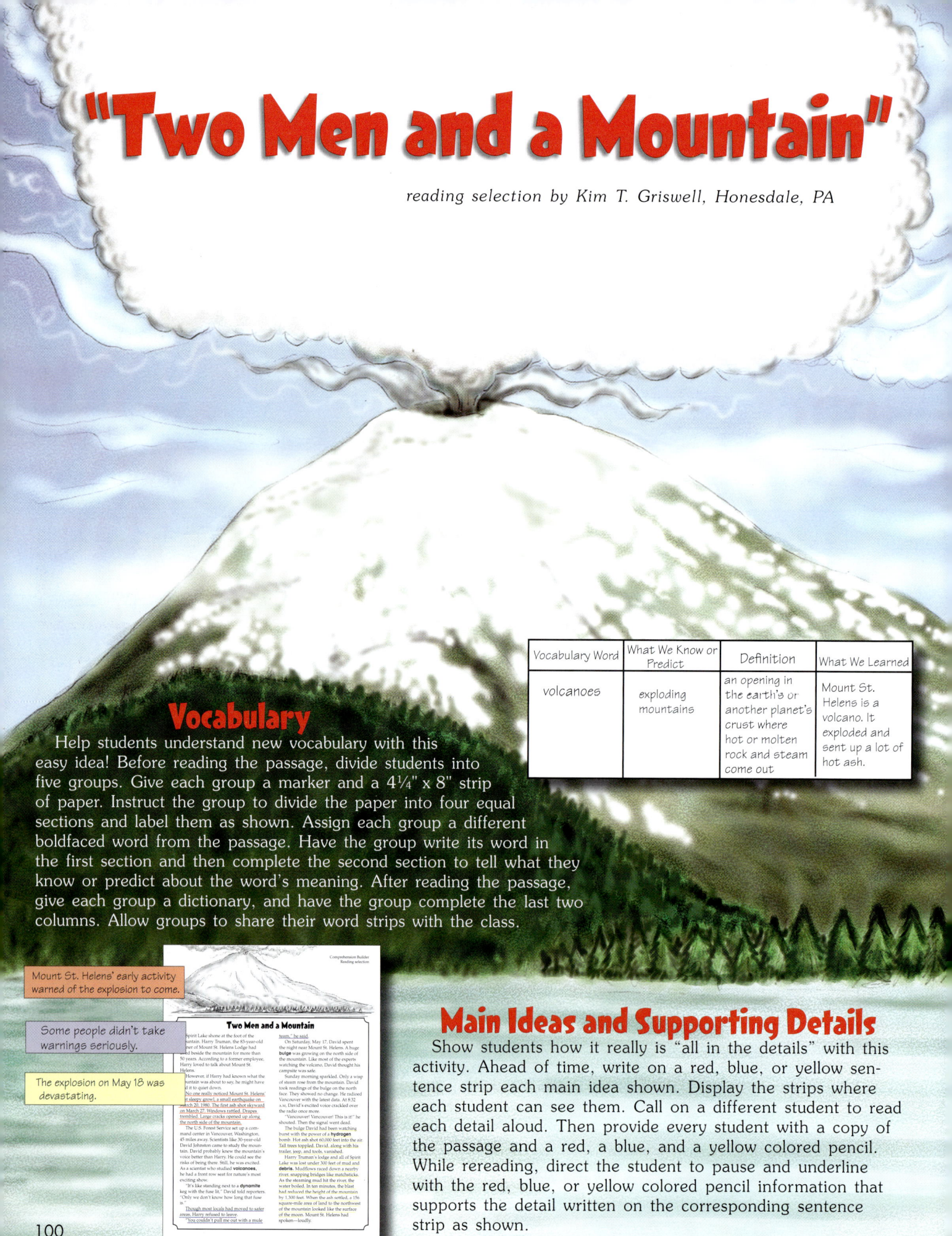

"Two Men and a Mountain"

reading selection by Kim T. Griswell, Honesdale, PA

Vocabulary

Help students understand new vocabulary with this easy idea! Before reading the passage, divide students into five groups. Give each group a marker and a 4¼" x 8" strip of paper. Instruct the group to divide the paper into four equal sections and label them as shown. Assign each group a different boldfaced word from the passage. Have the group write its word in the first section and then complete the second section to tell what they know or predict about the word's meaning. After reading the passage, give each group a dictionary, and have the group complete the last two columns. Allow groups to share their word strips with the class.

Vocabulary Word	What We Know or Predict	Definition	What We Learned
volcanoes	exploding mountains	an opening in the earth's or another planet's crust where hot or molten rock and steam come out	Mount St. Helens is a volcano. It exploded and sent up a lot of hot ash.

Main Ideas and Supporting Details

Show students how it really is "all in the details" with this activity. Ahead of time, write on a red, blue, or yellow sentence strip each main idea shown. Display the strips where each student can see them. Call on a different student to read each detail aloud. Then provide every student with a copy of the passage and a red, a blue, and a yellow colored pencil. While rereading, direct the student to pause and underline with the red, blue, or yellow colored pencil information that supports the detail written on the corresponding sentence strip as shown.

- Mount St. Helens' early activity warned of the explosion to come.
- Some people didn't take warnings seriously.
- The explosion on May 18 was devastating.

Personification

This activity shows students why Mount St. Helens seemed like such a character. Tell students that the author of "Two Men and a Mountain" used *personification* to give human characteristics to the mountain. Next, provide each student with a 4½" x 9" piece of white construction paper. Direct her to divide the paper into three equal-size sections as shown. Have her write the provided captions in the first and last boxes. (Remind the student that the text is in quotation marks because it comes directly from the passage.) Then direct the student to illustrate a cartoon that corresponds with each caption. For the middle panel, have the student create a caption that personifies Mount St. Helens during the eruption and then illustrate her caption. If desired, post the completed cartoons on a board titled "Mount St. Helens—Personified."

"No one really noticed Mount St. Helens' first sleepy growl…" | Angrily, the mountain spit out a column of ash. | "Mount St. Helens had spoken—loudly."

Drawing Conclusions

Enhance students' ability to draw conclusions about a volcano's danger with this art activity! To begin, invite a volunteer to read aloud the last two paragraphs of the passage on page 102. Have students brainstorm a list of four or five warnings that could be posted about the possible outcome of a volcanic eruption. Then divide students into small groups. Give each group a sheet of construction paper and markers or crayons. Direct the group to select an idea from the brainstormed list and then use it to make a poster warning about the dangers of an active volcano. Provide time for students to share their posters; then display their completed work as evidence of understanding.

WARNING: If this volcano explodes, hot ash could shoot 60,000 feet into the air!

Careful! The lake might be boiling!

DANGER of Debris Falling!

Two Men and a Mountain

Spirit Lake shone at the foot of the mountain. Harry Truman, the 83-year-old owner of Mount St. Helens Lodge, had lived beside the mountain for more than 50 years. According to a former employee, Harry loved to talk to and about Mount St. Helens.

However, if Harry had known what the mountain was about to say, he might have told it to quiet down.

No one really noticed Mount St. Helens' first sleepy growl, a small earthquake on March 20, 1980. The first ash shot skyward on March 27. Windows rattled. Drapes trembled. Large cracks opened up along the north side of the mountain.

The U.S. Forest Service set up a command center in Vancouver, Washington, 45 miles away. Scientists like 30-year-old David Johnston came to study the mountain. David probably knew the mountain's voice better than Harry. He could see the risks of being there. Still, he was excited. As a scientist who studied **volcanoes,** he had a front row seat for nature's most exciting show.

"It's like standing next to a **dynamite** keg with the fuse lit," David told reporters. "Only we don't know how long that fuse is."

Though most locals had moved to safer areas, Harry refused to leave.

"You couldn't pull me out with a mule team," he said.

On Saturday, May 17, David spent the night near Mount St. Helens. A huge **bulge** was growing on the north side of the mountain. Like most of the experts watching the volcano, David thought his campsite was safe.

Sunday morning sparkled. Only a wisp of steam rose from the mountain. David took readings of the bulge on the north face. They showed no change. He radioed Vancouver with the latest data. At 8:32 A.M., David's excited voice crackled over the radio once more.

"Vancouver! Vancouver! This is it!" he shouted. Then the signal went dead.

The bulge David had been watching burst with the power of a **hydrogen** bomb. Hot ash shot 60,000 feet into the air. Tall trees toppled. David, along with his trailer, jeep, and tools, vanished.

Harry Truman's lodge and all of Spirit Lake were lost under 300 feet of mud and **debris.** Mudflows raced down a nearby river, snapping bridges like matchsticks. As the steaming mud hit the river, the water boiled. In ten minutes, the blast had reduced the height of the mountain by 1,300 feet. When the ash settled, a 156 square-mile area of land to the northwest of the mountain looked like the surface of the moon. Mount St. Helens had spoken—loudly.

"Without Warning"

reading selection by Kim T. Griswell, Honesdale, PA
activities by Kim Minafo, Cary, NC

Compare and Contrast

While reading the selection, did students notice differences between weather forecasting and communication today and in 1900? Draw a T chart on the chalkboard, labeling one side "1900" and the other side with this year's date. Then challenge students to scan the selection and identify details related to 1900, such as chalk maps that had to be updated by hand or people getting warnings by word of mouth. On the right side, have students give contrasting details that describe things today, such as computers tracking the weather or people seeing warnings on the Internet. Also encourage students to add other details from their prior knowledge about how weather forecasting and communication have changed over the years.

Cause and Effect

Have students determine cause-and-effect relationships in the story with the following activity. Begin by explaining that the *effect* is what happens and the *cause* is why something happens. List cause-and-effect clue words on the chalkboard (such as *because, since, when, so, then, as a result of,* and *therefore*). Then guide students in picking an event that happened in the passage and using the clue words to create a cause-and-effect statement (see statements shown). Next, pair students and provide each pair with two 3" x 12" blue construction paper strips; have them cut across the top of the strips as illustrated. Instruct the pair to identify other events and write statements on its own, using the clue words. Finally, bring on a bigger wave of cause-and-effect practice by inviting each set of students to present its sentences and ask classmates to identify which part of each is the cause or the effect.

No one guessed how bad the storm would be <u>because</u> people thought the city wasn't in any danger.

<u>Since</u> water was rising fast, Cline sent a warning to the Weather Bureau.

Drawing Conclusions

Give your students practice drawing conclusions with this after-reading activity. First, explain to students that readers must draw conclusions or use details and personal experiences to determine things that are not in the reading. In small groups, ask students to conclude lessons that they or those from the story could learn. Then instruct the group to scan the selection for evidence that supports its conclusion.

Next, give each student a six-inch red square and a four-inch black square cut from construction paper. Also give him access to a glue stick and a white colored pencil. Have each student write his favorite conclusion and supporting story detail on the black square as shown. Then have him glue the square in the center of the red paper to make a flag. Display each student's flag in a set, as shown, to resemble a hurricane warning. Title the display "WARNING: A Hurricane of Conclusions."

Conclusion: Always take weather warnings seriously.
Story Detail: The Cubans told about the storm, but the Americans didn't believe them.

Conclusion: Never think that something can't happen to you.
Story Detail: No one thought the city was in real danger.

Summarizing

Sum up your study of the selection by having students recount the event in the form of a modern-day news report. Begin by leading the class in a discussion of the important events mentioned in the selection. Make a list of the events on the board. Then divide students into groups of three. Have each group use the class list to help develop a breaking news report script, complete with pictures from the scene (student drawings). Invite each set of reporters to present its news broadcast to students in another class.

Without Warning

In 1900, the city of Galveston shone like a Texas star. With its pretty beaches and warm sea breezes, it was a nice place to live or visit. Though storms at times blew in off the sea, no one thought the city was in real danger.

Isaac Cline, a local meteorologist, thought that the city was safe from huge storms. In this day, meteorology was a young science. People like Cline worked for the U.S. Weather Bureau. They tracked things such as temperature, rainfall, and wind patterns. They used chalk to draw the information on maps and then used the maps to tell the weather. Unfortunately, the maps couldn't help tell where storms were headed.

On September 5, word had been sent from Cuba to let Americans know about a hurricane. The Weather Bureau thought the Cubans were wrong. The bureau did not warn people.

The storm went by Key West, Florida. Then it turned toward Galveston. The wind caused waves that looked like long, easy swells. No one guessed what they would do when they hit the coast.

On September 8, the morning sky was different. It was pink and shone like a pearl. Cline went to the beach. The waves hit a bridge over the bay. They smacked the pillars and threw water over the rails. Cline timed the waves. He knew a storm was on the way. He went to his office to check his weather tools. From the window, he saw water start to rise. At first, it rose in the streets near the beach. But when the bay began to rise on one side of the city and the gulf on the other, Cline sent a warning to the bureau.

"Gulf rising rapidly; half the city now under water," it said.

He warned people up and down the coast.

Cline went home before the water rose too high. On the way, he warned those he saw. By the time Cline got home, water was up to his waist. The wind came in gusts that could knock a person down.

After a while, all he could see from his front door was water and tops of tall houses or poles. Behind his house was something more frightening. A tall wall of smashed homes was being pushed by the sea, hitting things in its path. When the wall hit Cline's house, his home went into the water.

More than 6,000 people lost their lives in the storm. The city was ruined. Cline, who lived, did not want a storm to surprise people again. He led the first scientific study of hurricanes in the United States.

Name _____ Identifying answers in text

Tracking Details

Read each sentence.
Select the *best* word that completes the sentence.
(Use details from the passage to help you.)
Write the matching letter on the line.

1. The storm went past Key West and turned ____ Galveston.

2. In 1900, meteorology was a(n) ____ science.

3. No one ____ what the waves would do.

4. Cline saw the water level ____.

5. Galveston had pretty beaches and ____ breezes.

6. Isaac went home ____ the water rose too high.

7. On September 8, the sky was ____ from other mornings.

8. Cline sent a warning about the gulf rising ____.

9. The water at Cline's home was ____ to his waist.

10. Cline led the ____ scientific study of hurricanes in the United States.

A. away
B. like
C. slowly
D. toward
E. rise
F. old
G. down
H. new
I. after
J. cool
K. rapidly
L. knew
M. fall
N. warm
O. different
P. up
Q. last
R. first
S. before
T. guessed

What do people near the western Pacific Ocean call storms like the one that hit Galveston?
To find out, match a letter to each numbered line below.

__ Y __ __ __ __ __ __
3   9 2 7 7 5 6

Bonus Box: Write a paragraph to describe a storm that you've been in.

Nonfiction Comprehension Builders • ©The Mailbox® Books • TEC61201 • Key p. 111

106   Note to the teacher: Use with the reading selection on page 105.

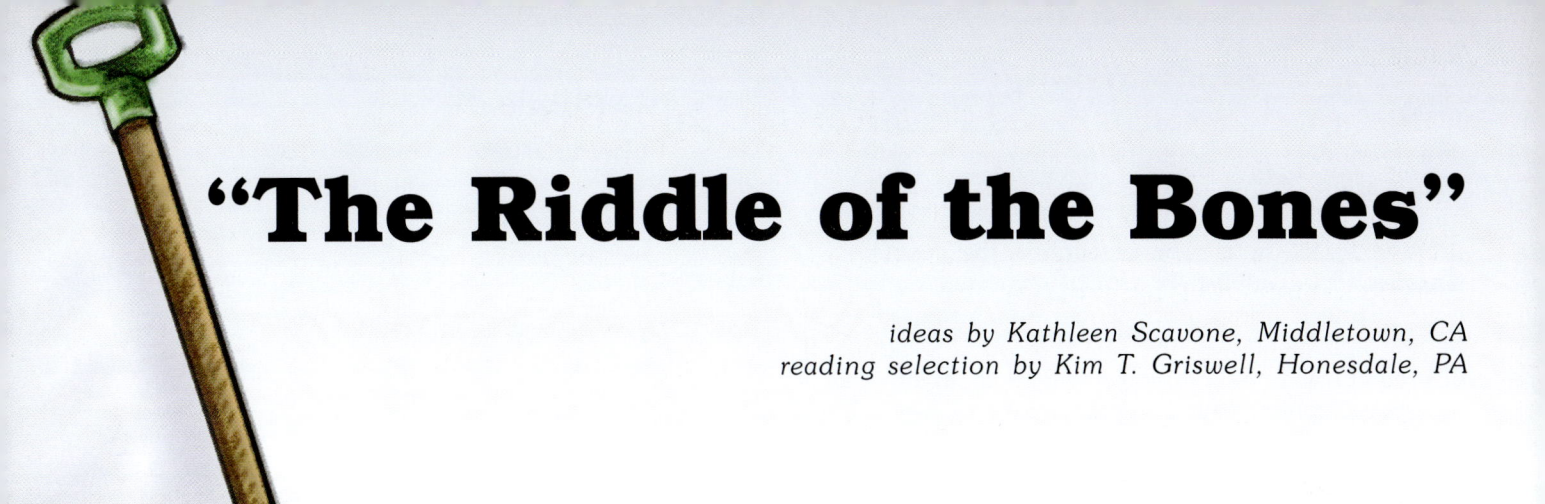

"The Riddle of the Bones"

ideas by Kathleen Scavone, Middletown, CA
reading selection by Kim T. Griswell, Honesdale, PA

Making Predictions
Before reading, initiate students' interest in the passage by giving them practice making predictions. Make a transparency of page 109. Display the title and first paragraph of the transparency—being sure to cover the art and remaining text with paper. After reading the visible information aloud, pair students and give each pair a sheet of white paper. Direct the twosome to fold its paper into three sections and label each section as shown. In the first section, have the pair list predictions about what might happen next. Then reveal the complete transparency and invite student volunteers to complete the reading. After reading, have pairs complete the second section of their papers by listing any evidence from the passage that confirms their predictions and the third section by revising any predictions that are not supported by the text.

The Riddle of the Bones
Predictions   Confirmations   Revisions

ancient
expedition
fossils
mammoth
mastodon

Vocabulary
Excavate key vocabulary words to help students better understand what they read! Write each boldfaced word from the selection on page 109 on a bone-shaped cutout. Display the words where every student can see them. Then challenge the students to look up each word and use it in a sentence. Set aside time for a few students to share sentences for each word. Have the class vote on the sentence that best helps them remember the meaning of the word. Direct the student who wrote the sentence to write it on the board, mounting the corresponding bone cutout in the appropriate part of the sentence.

Summarizing

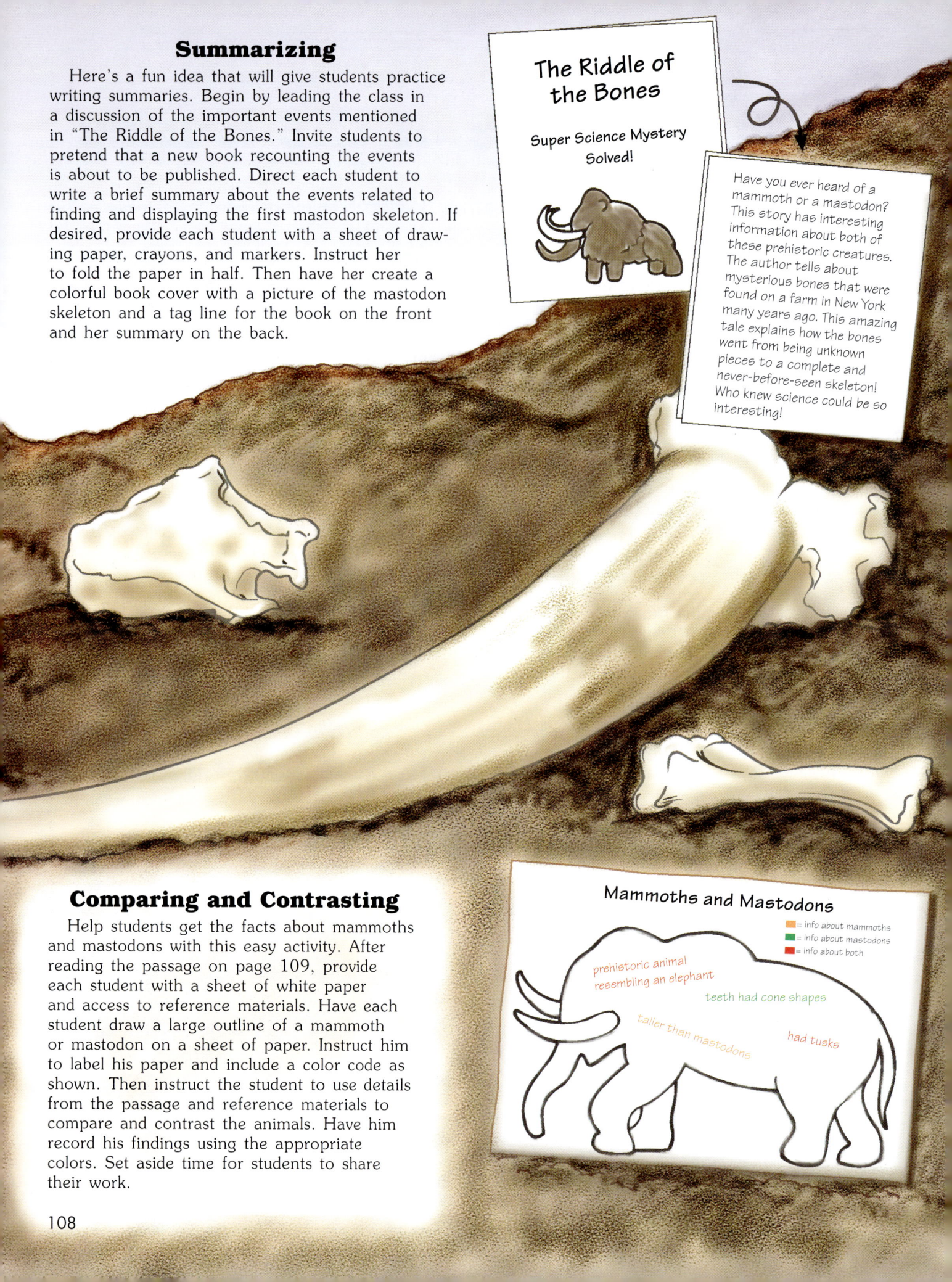

Here's a fun idea that will give students practice writing summaries. Begin by leading the class in a discussion of the important events mentioned in "The Riddle of the Bones." Invite students to pretend that a new book recounting the events is about to be published. Direct each student to write a brief summary about the events related to finding and displaying the first mastodon skeleton. If desired, provide each student with a sheet of drawing paper, crayons, and markers. Instruct her to fold the paper in half. Then have her create a colorful book cover with a picture of the mastodon skeleton and a tag line for the book on the front and her summary on the back.

The Riddle of the Bones
Super Science Mystery Solved!

Have you ever heard of a mammoth or a mastodon? This story has interesting information about both of these prehistoric creatures. The author tells about mysterious bones that were found on a farm in New York many years ago. This amazing tale explains how the bones went from being unknown pieces to a complete and never-before-seen skeleton! Who knew science could be so interesting!

Comparing and Contrasting

Help students get the facts about mammoths and mastodons with this easy activity. After reading the passage on page 109, provide each student with a sheet of white paper and access to reference materials. Have each student draw a large outline of a mammoth or mastodon on a sheet of paper. Instruct him to label his paper and include a color code as shown. Then instruct the student to use details from the passage and reference materials to compare and contrast the animals. Have him record his findings using the appropriate colors. Set aside time for students to share their work.

Mammoths and Mastodons

= info about mammoths
= info about mastodons
= info about both

prehistoric animal resembling an elephant
teeth had cone shapes
taller than mastodons
had tusks

The Riddle of the Bones

In a marshy field on a farm in New York, **ancient** bones were hidden under the soil. By the time a farmer found them, some easily crumbled to dust and others had turned to stone. The bones were huge—monstrous! What kind of creature could have left behind such bones?

Native American legends told of huge creatures that once roamed the land. They killed the deer, elk, and bison. They destroyed homes. The Great Man who lived above hurled lightening bolts. He wiped out all of the monstrous animals except one. Could the bones belong to one of these ancient animals?

Charles Willson Peale decided to find out. Peale had founded America's first natural history museum. He heard that hip bones, a tusk, and parts of a skull had been dug up by the farmer. Maybe the huge bones belonged to a **mammoth** such as those found in Kentucky and Siberia. So far, no one had found enough mammoth bones to make a complete skeleton. If enough could be found, Peale could display a skeleton in his museum.

Leading a scientific **expedition,** Peale headed to New York State. He could not believe the number of bones the farmer had collected. Among the **fossils,** he found a five-foot-long piece of curved tusk. What a find!

Peale hired local men and boys to help dig. They dug through layer after layer of earth. They hacked through thick yellow roots, shoveled out ashy soil, and scooped up decayed shells. The more they dug, the more fossils they found. Workers found nearly everything Peale needed to complete his skeleton—except a jawbone.

Peale kept searching for the missing piece of this mammoth puzzle. Finally, he found the lower jawbone. It weighed more than 60 pounds!

With jawbone in hand, Peale now had enough fossils to make the skeleton of the beast. He sent the bones by stagecoach to his museum in Philadelphia. Over a period of three months, he and his aides fastened the fossils with plaster of paris and wire. He filled in gaps with bones carved from wood. He had no idea what the finished animal would look like until it stood before him at last.

When Peale opened his display to the public, he called the beast a mammoth. It stood 11 feet tall from shoulders to feet. It was 15 feet long from chin to rump. It had curved, ten-foot-long tusks. Because its teeth had cone shapes, unlike a mammoth's flat teeth, a French scientist called the beast a **mastodon.**

Though Peale solved one riddle, another remains. Why did the mastodons vanish? Only time and science will tell.

Answer Keys

Page 12
1. O
2. K
3. A
4. W
5. D
6. R
7. L
8. E
9. H
10. Y

The skater WORKED "WHEEL-Y" HARD!

Page 16

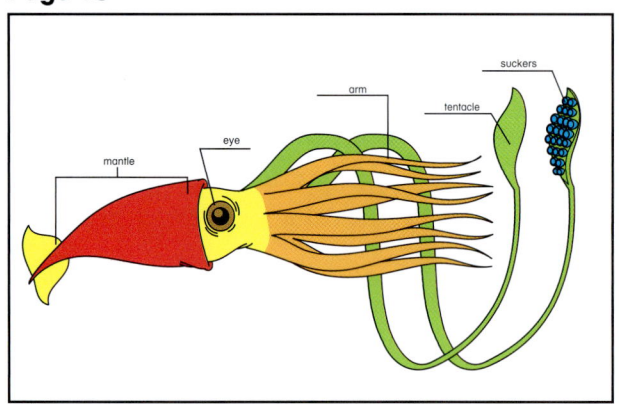

(Diagram of a squid with labels: mantle, eye, arm, tentacle, suckers)

Page 28
1. A
2. S
3. T
4. E
5. G
6. Z
7. R
8. F

FREEZE TAG

Page 30

small	as small as a fingernail about three inches long
colorful	red, orange, green, yellow, blue
poison	ooze poison onto their skin tastes bad can make animals sick
darts	rub their darts on the frogs' skin use the poison darts to hunt

Page 36
I. Ants can wiggle their antennae to send a message.
II. Ants can use sound to send a message.
   A. Some ants tap on nest walls to send messages.
   B. Some ants squeak or buzz.
III. Ants leave chemical trails that send messages.

Page 41
Answers may vary.
1. Draw a shape for the face.
2. Draw guidelines that show where to put the eyes, the ears, a nose, and a mouth.
3. Make one part of the face stand out. Make it bigger or smaller.
4. Keep sketching to add details and make the cartoon character's face.
5. Make the parts that you like darker until you are finished drawing your cartoon character.
6. Name your character.

Page 49
1. I
2. S
3. H
4. P
5. C

CHIPS!

Page 53
1. t
2. u
3. i
4. e
5. p
6. o
7. r
8. s

If someone always follows a game-day routine, you might say that person is superstitious.

Page 57

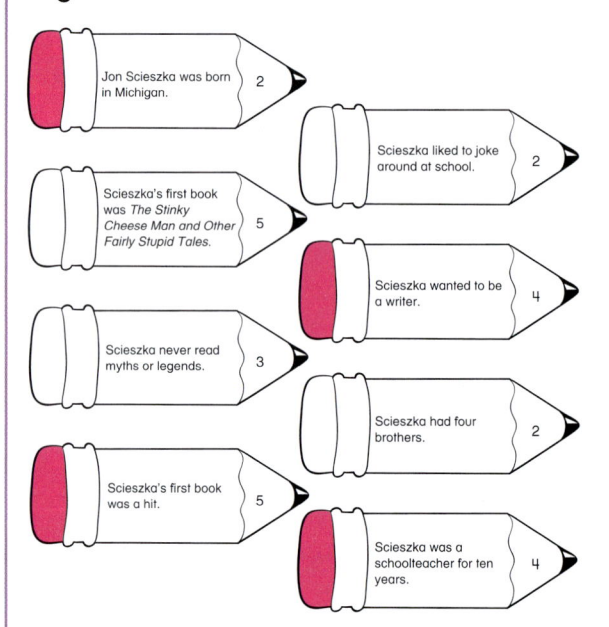

- Jon Scieszka was born in Michigan. — 2
- Scieszka liked to joke around at school. — 2
- Scieszka's first book was *The Stinky Cheese Man and Other Fairly Stupid Tales*. — 5
- Scieszka wanted to be a writer. — 4
- Scieszka never read myths or legends. — 3
- Scieszka had four brothers. — 2
- Scieszka's first book was a hit. — 5
- Scieszka was a schoolteacher for ten years. — 4

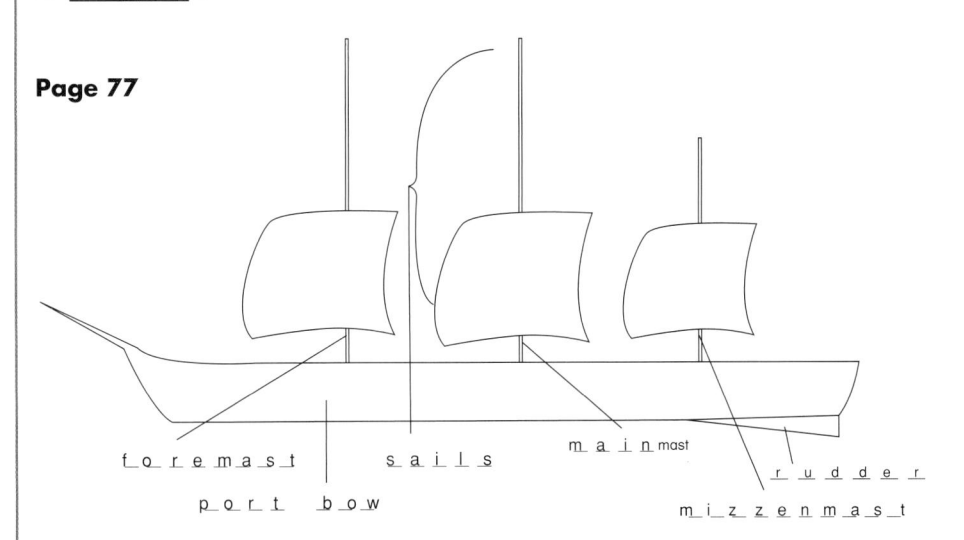

Page 61
1. A shark can see very well in dark water.
2. If a shark loses a tooth, it grows a new tooth to replace it.
3. To smell, a shark uses almost one-third of its brain.
4. A shark's heart is very small.
5. Sharks swim most of the time to keep from sinking.
6. A shark's liver holds oil and fat that help the shark float.

Page 65
fin: a part of a fish's body that sticks out and is used to swim and to steer
piranha: a freshwater fish with very sharp teeth
prey: an animal that another animal hunts for food
scales: thin, hard pieces that cover fish
scatter: to spread something out
school of fish: a large group of the same kind of fish that swim together

Page 69
1. The *Whydah* leaves England on its first trip.
2. During the *Whydah*'s second trip, two pirate ships chase it.
3. Black Sam and his crew capture the *Whydah*.
4. Pirates use the *Whydah* to rob other ships.
5. The *Whydah* hits a bad storm, and it sinks.
6. Sand buries the wrecked ship and its riches.
7. Divers find three cannons that were on the *Whydah*.
8. Treasure hunters find over 100,000 items from the *Whydah*.

Page 73
1. O
2. T
3. N
4. M
5. R
6. S
A "MON-STAR"!

Page 77
foremast, sails, main mast, rudder, port bow, mizzenmast

Page 92
Category headings will vary. Accept reasonable responses.

Type of Animal	Where It Lives	What It Eats	Animal Color	How It Hides
chameleon	in the forest	insects	green	changes to brown or other colors quickly
flounder	in the sea	snails, shrimp	not given	changes to match bottom of sea or harbor, may show spots or stripes
ermine	field, woods, bushes	fish, mice, eggs	mainly brown	turns white to blend with snow
peppered moth	forest or city	not given	white, gray, or dark in color	has changed color over time to match its environment
walking stick	trees, bushes	not given	green or brown	uses its shape to look like a twig or leaf

Bonus Box: Responses will vary. However, students should indicate that in order to categorize, one must look for ways things are alike and sort them into groups.

Page 106
1. D
2. H
3. T
4. E
5. N
6. S
7. O
8. K
9. P
10. R
TYPHOONS

Skills Index

Activating prior knowledge, 4, 7, 17, 20, 25, 33, 58, 61, 85

Answering multiple-choice questions, 49, 53, 73

Answering open-ended questions, 75

Author's purpose, 81, 84, 93

Building background knowledge, 13, 16, 70, 74, 77

Categorizing, 89, 92

Cause and effect, 94, 103

Citing text evidence, 30

Comparing and contrasting, 4, 7, 21, 24, 90, 103, 108

Completing an outline, 33, 36

Compound words, 8

Connecting fiction and nonfiction, 43

Context clues, 21, 22, 25, 50

Critical thinking, 55

Drawing conclusions, 79, 101, 104

Fact and opinion, 9, 12, 26, 59, 63, 78, 86

Finding answers in text, 57

Fluency, 14, 39

Following directions, 18

High-frequency words, 9, 11

Identifying answers in text, 106

Identifying important details, 51, 96

Inferring, 18, 67

Main idea, 47, 58, 100

Making connections, 26, 46

Making judgments, 94

Making predictions, 42, 45, 66, 81, 107

Monitoring comprehension, 66

Paraphrasing, 34, 39, 41

Personification, 101

Point of view, 63, 97

Proper names, 54

Questioning, 22, 55, 62, 86

Reading for details, 85, 88, 90

Reading purpose, 8, 38

Recalling details, 28

Rhymes, 5

Sequencing, 69, 96

Skimming, 14

Spelling, 32

Summarizing, 5, 43, 47, 59, 79, 82, 104, 108

Supporting details, 47, 75, 100

Syllabication, 67

Synonyms, 34, 37, 97, 99

Synthesizing, 71

Text features, 29

Visualizing, 13, 29, 50, 71

Vocabulary, 17, 38, 42, 43, 46, 54, 62, 65, 70, 78, 82, 89, 93, 100, 107

Writing a legend, 74

Writing a narrative, 14